BLACK & DECKER®

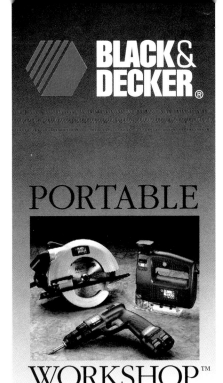

PORTABLE

WORKSHOP™

*Basic Wood Projects
with Portable Power Tools*

Den &
Family Room
Furnishings

Credits

Copyright © 1996
Cowles Creative Publishing, Inc.
Formerly Cy DeCosse Incorporated
5900 Green Oak Drive
Minnetonka, Minnesota 55343
1-800-328-3895
Printed in U.S.A.

A Division of Cowles Enthusiast Media, Inc.

President/COO: Nino Tarantino
Executive V.P./Editor-in-Chief: William B. Jones

Executive Editor: Paul Currie
Project Director: Mark Johanson
Associate Creative Director: Tim Himsel
Managing Editor: Kristen Olson
Project Manager: Lori Holmberg
Lead Project Designer: Jim Huntley
Editors: Mark Biscan, Andrew Sweet
Editor & Technical Artist: Jon Simpson
Art Director: Gina Seeling
Technical Production Editor: Greg Pluth
Project Designer & Technical Checker: Rob Johnstone
Technical Art Draftsman: John T. Drigot
Vice President of Photography & Production: Jim Bindas
Copy Editor: Janice Cauley
Shop Supervisor: Phil Juntti
Lead Builder: Rob Johnstone
Builders: Troy Johnson, John Nadeau
Production Staff: Carol Harvatin, Laura Hokkanen, Tom Hoops, Guy Messenger, Mike Schauer, Brent Thomas, Kay Wethern
Studio Services Manager: Marcia Chambers
Photo Services Coordinator: Cheryl Neisen
Lead Photographer: Rebecca Schmitt
Photography Assistant: Greg Wallace
Production Manager: Stasia Dorn

Printed on American paper by:
 Inland Press 99 98 97 96 / 5 4 3 2 1

President/COO: Philip L. Penny

Created by: The Editors of Cowles Creative Publishing, Inc., in cooperation with Black & Decker.
● **BLACK&DECKER** is a trademark of the Black & Decker Corporation and is used under license.

Library of Congress
Cataloging-in-Publication Data

Den & family room furnishings.
        p. cm.—(Portable workshop)
   At head of title: Black & Decker.
   ISBN   0-86573-675-8 (hardcover).

1. Furniture making--Amateurs' manuals.
I. Cy DeCosse Incorporated.
II. Black & Decker Corporation (Towson, MD)
III. Series.
TT195.D46   1996
684.1--dc20   96-24048

Contents

Introduction

In today's fast-paced, often stressful world, few pleasures compare with retreating to the security and comfort of a warm, friendly den or a lively, energetic family room. There you can put the day behind you and delight, for awhile, in the activities you and your loved ones most enjoy. You turn to the family room to unwind in a casual setting with friends, share snacks, play a game, take in a favorite show and fill the air with laughter. You retire to the sanctuary of your den for simple peace and quiet, or to let a treasured book or a letter to a friend restore your spirit. In *Den & Family Room Furnishings* from the Black & Decker® Portable Workshop™, you'll find a showcase of projects that help you turn your den and family room into havens for leisure-time living.

Using just a few simple tools, you can build a pine futon frame the whole family can snuggle into; a classic library table for your den; a poker table for evenings full of congenial competition; an oak stepladder for reaching top shelves; a writing desk, drafting stool and secretary topper that can be made individually or as a set; and many other furnishings to give your den or family room personal charm and functional appeal.

For each of the creative, practical building projects in *Den & Family Room Furnishings*, you will find a complete cutting list of parts, a materials-shopping list, a detailed construction drawing, full-color photographs of the major construction steps and easy-to-follow directions that guide you through every step of the building process.

The Black & Decker® Portable Workshop™ book series gives weekend do-it-yourselfers the power to build beautiful wood projects. All projects can be made with just a few basic hand-held power tools, using common building materials sold at any building center. Ask your local bookseller for more information on other volumes in this innovative new series.

NOTICE TO READERS

This book provides useful instructions, but we cannot anticipate all of your working conditions or the characteristics of your materials and tools. For safety, you should use caution, care, and good judgment when following the procedures described in this book. Consider your own skill level and the instructions and safety precautions associated with the various tools and materials shown. Neither the publisher nor Black & Decker® can assume responsibility for any damage to property, injury to persons, or losses incurred as a result of misuse of the information provided.

Organizing Your Worksite

Portable power tools and hand tools offer a level of convenience that is a great advantage over stationary power tools. But using them safely and conveniently requires some basic housekeeping. Whether you are working in a garage, a basement or outdoors, it is important that you establish a flat, dry holding area where you can store tools. Set aside a piece of plywood on sawhorses, or dedicate an area of your workbench for tool storage, and be sure to return tools to that area once you are finished with them. If you are working outdoors, be sure to use a grounded (GFCI) extension cord for your power tools.

It is also important that all waste, including lumber scraps and sawdust, be disposed of in a timely fashion. Check with your local waste disposal department before throwing away any large scraps of building materials or any finishing-material containers.

> *Safety Tips*
> *•Always wear eye and hearing protection when operating power tools and performing any other dangerous activities.*
> *•Choose a well-ventilated work area when cutting or shaping wood and when using finishing products.*

Tools & Materials

At the start of each project, you will find a set of symbols that show which power tools are used to complete the project as it is shown (see below). You will also need a set of basic hand tools: a hammer, screwdrivers, tape measure, a level, a combination square, C-clamps, and pipe or bar clamps. You also will find a shopping list of all the construction materials you will need. Miscellaneous materials and hardware are listed with the cutting list that accompanies the construction drawing. When buying lumber, note that the "nominal" size of the lumber is usually larger than the "actual size." For example, a 2 × 4 is actually 1½ × 3½".

Power Tools You Will Use

Circular saw *to make straight cuts. For long cuts and rip-cuts, use a straight-edge guide. Install a carbide-tipped combination blade for most projects.*

Drills: *use a cordless drill for drilling pilot holes and counterbores, and to drive screws; use an electric drill for sanding and grinding tasks.*

Jig saw *for making contoured cuts and internal cuts. Use a combination wood blade for most projects where you will cut pine, cedar or plywood.*

Power sander *to prepare wood for a finish and to smooth out sharp edges. Owning several power sanders (⅓-sheet, ¼-sheet) is helpful.*

Belt sander *for resurfacing rough wood. Can also be used as a stationary sander when mounted on its side on a flat worksurface.*

Router *to cut decorative edges and roundovers in wood. As you gain more experience, use routers for cutting grooves (like dadoes) to form joints.*

Guide to Building Materials Used in This Book

•Sheet goods:
PLYWOOD: *Basic sheet good sold in several grades (from CDX to AB) and thicknesses. Inexpensive to moderate.*
BIRCH PLYWOOD: *A workable, readily available alternative to pine or fir plywood. Has smooth surface excellent for painting or staining; few voids in the edges. Moderately expensive.*
OAK PLYWOOD: *Oak-veneered plywood commonly sold in ¾" and ¼" thicknesses. Fairly expensive.*
LAUAN PLYWOOD: *Usually ¼" to ½" thick, found in cabinetry and furniture, and used as a flooring underlay. Inexpensive.*
TILEBOARD: *Thin hardboard paneling with a water-resistant surface formed to look like grouted tiles. Inexpensive.*

•Dimension lumber:
PINE: *A basic softwood used for many interior projects. "Select" and "#2 or better" are suitable grades. Relatively inexpensive.*
RED OAK: *A common hardwood that stains well and is very durable. Relatively inexpensive.*
ASPEN: *A soft, workable hardwood. Available at building centers in standard sizes and in extra-wide glued panels. Moderate.*

Guide to Fasteners & Adhesives Used in This Book

•Fasteners & hardware:
WOOD SCREWS: *Brass or steel; most projects use screws with a #6 or #8 shank. Can be driven with a power driver.*
NAILS & BRADS: *Finish nails can be set below the wood surface: common (box) nails have wide, flat heads; brads or wire nails are very small, thin fasteners with small heads.*
Misc.: *Door pulls & knobs; butt hinges; lock hardware; decorative hinges; plastic or nylon furniture glides; magnetic door catches; roller catches; chest-lid supports; corner brackets; other specialty hardware as indicated.*

•Adhesives:
WOOD GLUE: *Yellow glue is suitable for all projects in this book.*
MOISTURE-RESISTANT WOOD GLUE: *Any exterior wood glue, such as plastic resin glue.*
THIN-SET MORTAR: *An adhesive used with ceramic tile.*

•Miscellaneous materials:
Wood plugs (for filling counterbores); ceramic tile & grout; dowel rods; lamp hardware kit; copper tubing.

Finishing Your Project

Glue pre-cut wood plugs into visible screw counterbores and sand them until smooth; fill nail holes and countersunk screw holes with wood putty, then sand smooth. Sand all surfaces to remove rough spots and splinters, using medium-grit (120 to 150) sandpaper. Wipe the wood clean with a rag dipped in mineral spirits, then prime and paint with enamel paint, or apply a wood-staining agent to color the wood. Topcoat with several coats of tung oil, polyurethane or other products as desired. Mask or remove hardware before applying finishing products.

Drafting Stool

Simple and sturdy, this oak beauty keeps your posture perfect as you work at your drafting table or writing desk.

Proper seating is the key to productivity and comfort at a writing desk, drafting table or any workstation. An ultra-soft reclining or swiveling chair can result in bad body position, sore muscles and a drowsy disposition. On the other hand, an unsupportive, rigid chair can make working at your desk uncomfortable and unpleasant. This drafting stool offers firm support without lulling you into slumped shoulders or sleep.

This drafting stool was designed for use with the writing desk (page 12). The design styles and scale of the stool and writing table match well. But you don't have to use this project with a drafting table. This solid oak stool can also be used as a bar stool in your den. You may even choose to use it in the kitchen at your breakfast counter. We used oak building materials, but you can select lumber to match your desk or room decor. We filled the screw counterbores with oak plugs, but contrasting plugs would provide an interesting design element. You have many fine options when building and using this drafting stool. Best of all, this stool is much easier to build than its appearance suggests.

CONSTRUCTION MATERIALS

Quantity	Lumber
3	1 × 2" × 8' oak
2	1 × 4" × 6' oak
2	2 × 2" × 8' oak

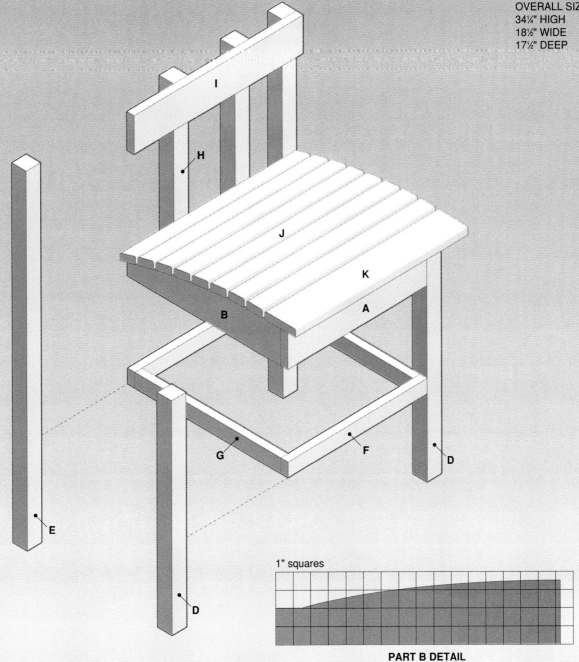

1" squares

PART B DETAIL

Key	Part	Dimension	Pcs.	Material
A	Front	¾ × 3½ × 15"	1	Oak
B	Side	¾ × 2 × 16¼"	2	Oak
C	Back	¾ × 3½ × 15"	1	Oak
D	Front leg	1½ × 1½ × 21¼"	2	Oak
E	Rear leg	1½ × 1½ × 34¼"	2	Oak
F	End rail	¾ × 1½ × 15"	2	Oak

Cutting List (left)

Key	Part	Dimension	Pcs.	Material
G	Side rail	¾ × 1½ × 15½"	2	Oak
H	Back brace	1½ × 1½ × 16½"	2	Oak
I	Backrest	¾ × 3½ × 18½"	1	Oak
J	Slat	¾ × 1½ × 18½"	8	Oak
K	Front slat	¾ × 3½ × 18½"	1	Oak

Cutting List (right)

Materials: Wood screws (#6 × 1⅝", #6 × 2"), wood glue, 10d finish nails, finishing materials.

Note: Measurements reflect the actual thickness of dimensional lumber.

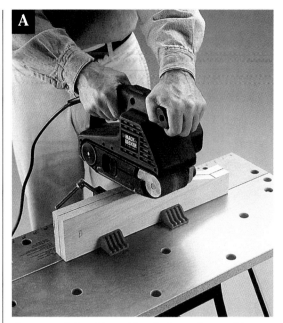

Gang-sand the sides with a belt sander, making sure their profiles are identical.

Align the seat frame on the top reference lines, and fasten it to the legs.

Directions: Drafting Stool

MAKE THE SEAT FRAME. The seat frame is the central structural element in the drafting stool. The frame is sloped from front to back, forming the seat shape. This slope is made by transferring cutting lines from a grid pattern on page 9 to the sides of the frame. Start by cutting the front (A), sides (B) and back (C) to size. Sand the parts to smooth out any rough edges. Draw a grid with 1" squares onto a face of a side board. (Use the *Part B Detail* from page 9 as a guide for drawing the side contour.) Cut the side to shape with a jig saw, and sand the edges. Trace the finished side onto the uncut side board, and cut it to shape. Clamp the sides together and gang-sand them with a belt sander **(photo A),** making sure their profiles are identical. Position the front board (A) against the front ends of the sides. Drill counterbored pilot holes, and fasten the front to the sides

with glue and #6 × 1⅝" wood screws. Make the counterbores deep enough to accept a ⅜"-dia. wood plug. Position the back board (C) between the sides so the rear face is 1½" in from the ends of the sides. Make sure the bottom edges of

the parts are flush, and fasten the back with glue and #6 × 1⅝" wood screws.

ATTACH THE LEGS. Two legs are attached to the front and back of the seat frame. Before attaching the frame and legs, draw accurate reference lines

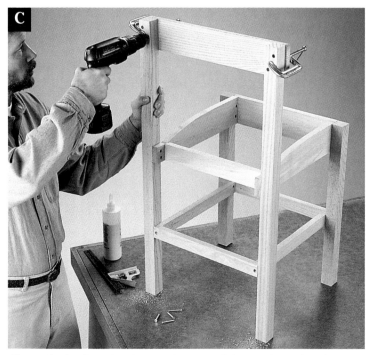

Clamp the backrest in place at the tops of the rear legs, then fasten with glue and wood screws.

Using 10d nails as spacers, fasten the seat slats to the top of the seat frame, ending with the front slat.

slightly off center. The front and rear edges of the rail assembly should be flush with the front and rear leg edges.

ATTACH THE BACK BRACES & BACKREST. Begin by cutting the back braces (H) and backrest (I) to size. Clamp the backrest to the fronts of the rear legs so the top edges are flush. The backrest should extend ¼" past the rear legs on both sides. Check the back of the legs for square, and drill staggered pilot holes with ½"-deep counterbores through the legs. Apply glue, and fasten the backrest to the rear legs with glue and #6 × 1⅝" wood screws **(photo C).** Attach the back braces to the back and backrest with glue and wood screws. Use a piece of 1 × 4 scrap as a spacer to maintain equal distance between the rear legs and back braces.

ATTACH THE SLATS. Cut the slats (J) and the front slat (K) to size. Sand the slats, slightly rounding the top edges with a belt sander. Starting at the rear of the seat, attach the slats with glue and counterbored #6 × 1⅝" wood screws. Maintain a ⅛"-wide gap between slats— 10d finish nails make good spacers. Clamp the front slat to the front of the seat frame with its front edge overhanging the front by ½" at the front and ¼" at each side. Attach the front slat with glue and counterbored screws **(photo D).**

APPLY FINISHING TOUCHES. Glue ⅜"-dia. wood plugs into all counterbores, and sand the plugs smooth so they are flush with the surface. Finish-sand all the surfaces with 180-grit sandpaper, and apply your finish of choice. We used three coats of tung oil.

to mark the position for the legs. Otherwise, the legs will be uneven. Start by cutting the front legs (D) and rear legs (E) to size. Sand the parts, then draw reference lines 8" and 17¾" up from the bottom ends. Position one front leg and one rear leg on your worksurface. Set the seat frame on the legs so the bottom edge is flush with the top reference lines. Apply glue and fasten the seat frame to the rear leg, keeping the ends flush and the frame square to the leg. Use counterbored #6 × 1⅝" wood screws, driven through the seat sides and into the leg. Make sure the seat frame is flush with the front edge of the front leg and with the top reference line. Drill pilot holes **(photo B),** and fasten the frame to the front leg with glue and wood screws. Turn the assembly over, and attach the remaining front leg

and rear leg, using the same methods.

ATTACH THE RAILS. The rails are joined together to form a simple frame. This frame is then attached between the legs to strengthen the stool. Cut the end rails (F) and side rails (G) to length. Position the side rails between the end rails so their top and bottom edges are flush. Drill counterbored pilot holes through the end rails, and use glue and #6 × 1⅝" wood screws to fasten the end rails to the side rails. Position the rail assembly between the posts so its bottom edges are flush with the bottom reference lines. Drill countersunk pilot holes through the side rails, and attach the rail assembly with glue and #6 × 1⅝" wood screws, driven through the side rails and into the legs. To avoid hitting the screws in the rail assembly, these screws must be

Writing Desk

Build this practical, attractive writing desk for a fraction of the cost of manufactured models.

CONSTRUCTION MATERIALS

Quantity	Lumber
1	¾" × 4 × 8' oak plywood
2	1 × 2" × 6' oak
2	1 × 4" × 6' oak
1	1 × 6" × 8' oak
1	1 × 10" × 6' oak
2	2 × 2" × 8' oak
1	¼" × 2 × 4' acrylic sheet
2	¾ × 1⅝" × 6' oak panel molding
2	⅜ × 1¹⁄₁₆" × 6' oak stop molding

A beautiful piece of furniture, this writing desk is based loosely on popular Shaker styling. With its hinged top, you have access to a storage area for keeping important papers organized and out of the way. We built the writing desk out of red oak, an attractive and long-lasting hardwood, so the project is sure to look great for a long time. Designed to be built as a set with the drafting stool and secretary top (pages 8, 66), the writing desk also works well as a stand-alone piece, and it can be built for a fraction of the cost of similar furnishings, even those sold by catalog. The writing surface is made from a clear acrylic sheet, giving you a smooth surface on which to write. When the acrylic sheet gets scratched or worn, just slip it out of the top frame and turn it over.

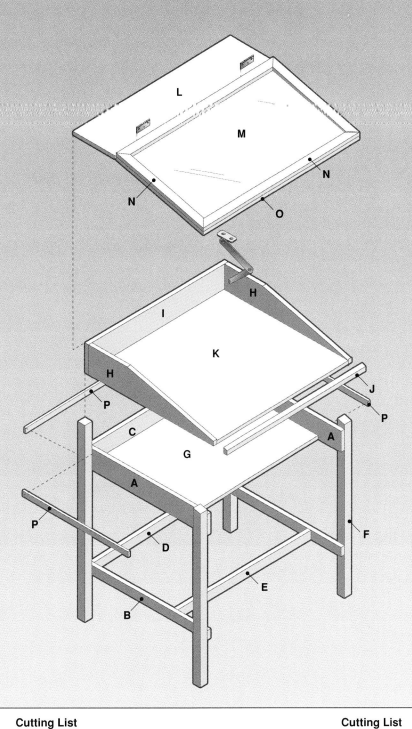

Cutting List

Key	Part	Dimension	Pcs.	Material
A	Apron side	¾ × 3½ × 24¾"	2	Oak
B	Side rail	¾ × 1½ × 24¾"	2	Oak
C	Apron back	¾ × 3½ × 30"	1	Oak
D	Back rail	¾ × 1½ × 30"	1	Oak
E	Kick rail	¾ × 1½ × 28½"	1	Oak
F	Leg	1½ × 1½ × 35¾"	4	Oak
G	Shelf	¾ × 20 × 28½"	1	Plywood
H	Desk side	¾ × 5½ × 26½"	2	Oak

Cutting List

Key	Part	Dimension	Pcs.	Material
I	Desk back	¾ × 5½ × 30"	1	Oak
J	Desk front	¾ × 1 × 30"	1	Oak
K	Desk bottom	¾ × 26½ × 28½"	1	Plywood
L	Desk top	¾ × 9¼ × 34"	1	Oak
M	Worksurface	¾ × 21 × 34"	1	Plywood
N	Top molding	¾ × 1⁵⁄₁₆ × *"	4	Panel molding
O	Top protector	¼ × 19⅛ × 32⅛"	1	Acrylic
P	Side trim	⅜ × 1¹⁄₁₆ × *"	3	Stop molding

Materials: Brass wood screws (#6 × 1¼", #6 × 1⅝", #6 × 2"), 1½ × 3" brass butt hinges, brass brads (¾", 1", 1½"), 6" heavy-duty lid-support hardware, oak veneer edge tape (25'), finishing materials.
Note: Measurements reflect the actual thickness of dimensional lumber.
*Cut to fit.

Fasten the apron assembly between the back legs with glue and wood screws, driven through the apron sides and into the legs.

Attach the front legs to the free ends of the aprons and rails.

Directions: Writing Desk

JOIN THE LEGS & APRON. Start by cutting the legs (F) to length. Sand the parts smooth. Set the legs together edge to edge with their ends flush. Draw reference lines across the legs, 8" and 30½" up from one end. These lines mark the positions of the apron and rail assemblies. To build the apron assembly, start by cutting the apron sides (A) and apron back (C) to length. Attach an apron side to each end of the apron back with glue and counterbored #6 × 2" wood screws, driven through the apron back and into the apron sides. Make sure the outside faces of the apron sides are flush with the ends of the apron back. To attach the apron assembly to the legs, first set a pair of legs on your worksurface, about 30" apart, with the reference lines facing each other. Position the assembly between the legs so the top edges of the assembly are flush

Use a block plane to trim the desk front to match the slanted profiles of the desk sides.

with the reference lines 30½" up from the bottom. Apply glue, and drill two counterbored pilot holes through the sides. Drive #6 × 1⅝" wood screws through the sides and into the legs **(photo A).** Avoid the screws already driven in the apron assembly.

INSTALL THE FRAME RAILS. The frame rails are 1 × 2 oak strips that fit between the legs to stabilize the desk. Cut the side rails (B), back rail (D) and kick rail (E) to length. Drill counterbored pilot holes, and attach the side rails to each end of the back rail with glue

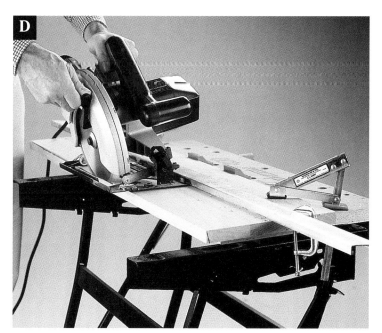

Use a circular saw and straightedge guide to make a slight bevel on the front edge of the desk top.

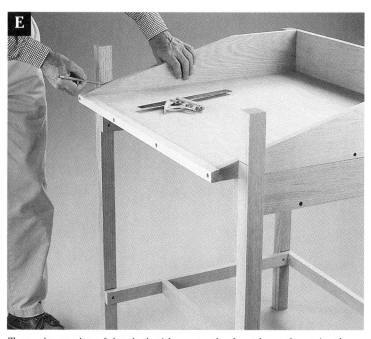

Trace the angles of the desk sides onto the front legs, then trim the legs to follow the sides.

bored pilot holes, and attach the rail assembly with glue and wood screws. Fasten the front legs to the fronts of the apron sides and side rails, making sure the reference lines are flush with the edges **(photo B).**

MAKE THE SHELF. The shelf fits within the apron assembly, flush with the bottom edges. Cut the shelf (G) to size. Sand the shelf to smooth out any rough edges. Apply oak veneer edge tape to one long edge of the shelf, using a household iron. Trim and sand the edges of the tape. Position the shelf between the apron sides so it butts against the inside face of the apron back. The front edge will be recessed 8" in from the front legs. Drill counterbored pilot holes, and attach the shelf to the aprons with glue and wood screws, driven through the apron sides and apron back. Make sure the taped edge of the shelf faces front. The shelf should be flush with the bottom edges of the apron assembly.

BUILD THE DESK BOX. The desk box is built as a unit, then installed on top of the aprons. Start by cutting the desk sides (H) to length. The desk sides are cut with slanted top edges. To make the slanted cuts, mark points on one long edge of each desk side, 8¼" in from one end. This long edge will be the top edge. Then draw reference lines on the opposite end of each side, 1" up from the bottom edge. Draw straight cutting

and #6 × 2" wood screws, driven through the back rail and into the side rail ends. Make sure the outside faces of the apron sides are flush with the ends of the apron back. Position the kick rail between the side rails so its front face is 7" in from the front ends of the

side rails. Make sure the top and bottom edges are flush, and attach the kick rail with glue and #6 × 2" wood screws. Position the rail assembly between the legs so the bottom edges are flush with the reference lines 8" up from the bottom of each leg. Drill counter-lines connecting the marks, and cut along the lines with a circular saw and straightedge cutting guide. Cut the desk back (I) to length from oak 1 × 6. Cut the desk bottom (K) from ¾"-thick plywood. To cut the 1"-thick desk front (J), use a straightedge cutting guide to rip-cut a 1"-thick strip from a 1 × 4 or 1 × 6. Sand to smooth out any rough spots. Drill counterbored pilot holes through the desk back, and use glue and #6 × 2" wood screws to fasten a desk side at each end, flush with the top, bottom and side edges of the desk back. Set the desk bottom between the desk sides, and attach it with glue and wood screws, driven through the desk sides and back and into the bottom. Drill counterbored pilot holes in the desk front, and fasten it to the front edge of the desk bottom. To trim the desk front to match the slanted profiles of the desk sides, first draw reference lines on each end of the desk front, extending the slanted profiles of the desk sides. Use a combination square to draw a reference line across the front face of the desk front, connecting the ends of the end reference lines. Use a block plane to trim the profile of the desk front to match the angles of the desk sides **(photo C).** To avoid damaging the desk sides with the plane, start the trimming with the block plane and finish with a pad sander.

MAKE THE DESK TOP. Cut the desk top (L) to size. The desk top has a bevel cut along one long edge where it meets the worksurface (M). To make this bevel, adjust the sole plate setting on a circular saw until it

Permanently fasten the top and side pieces of the frame around the worksurface.

cuts a ⅛"-deep bevel on the front edge of the desk top. First make test cuts on scrap pieces. Clamp a straightedge guide to the desk top, and make the bevel cut on one long edge of the workpiece, removing a ⅛"-thick strip **(photo D).**

INSTALL THE DESK BOX. Stand the leg assembly up, and slide the desk assembly into place on top of the side aprons, making sure the back edges are flush. In order for the desk top to sit flat on the desk sides, the front legs are cut to match the slanted profiles of the desk sides. First, trace the angles of the desk sides onto the front legs **(photo E).** Remove the desk assembly, and use a circular saw to cut the front legs along the cutting lines. Replace the desk, and make sure the front legs are cut at or slightly below the desk side profiles. Fasten the desk assembly with glue and #6 × 2" wood screws, driven through the desk sides and into the legs. Remember to

drill counterbored pilot holes before attaching the assemblies. Position the desk top on the flat section of the desk sides so the back edge of the desk top overhangs the back of the legs by ⅛". Make sure the beveled edge faces forward and slants in from top to bottom. Attach the desk top with glue and wood screws. Because there is a visible seam where the desk assembly meets the aprons, make the side trim (P) pieces that fit between the legs on the sides and back. Tack the side trim over the seam, using ¾" brass brads.

MAKE THE WORKSURFACE. The worksurface is a flat plywood board framed with molding. A sheet of clear acrylic is inserted in the molding frame to create a smooth writing surface. One piece of the molding is removable, allowing you to replace the acrylic if it gets worn and scratched. Cut the worksurface (M) to size. Apply veneer edge tape to all four

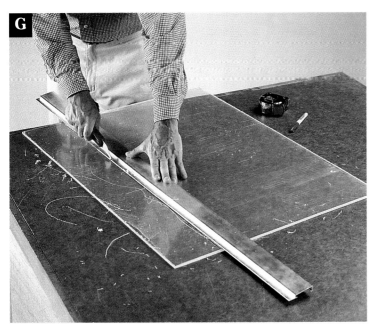

Score the acrylic sheet repeatedly, using a utility knife and a straightedge guide.

edges of the board. Sand to smooth out any rough edges. Cut the top molding (N) from ¾ × 1⁵⁄₁₆" panel molding to fit around the edges of the worksurface. Miter-cut the corners of the molding pieces to make miter joints. Use glue and ¾" brads to attach the top molding to the sides and top of the worksurface **(photo F).** Drive 1" brass brads through one molding piece and into the other at each joint, lock-nailing the pieces. To secure the unattached piece of top molding, first clamp it in place on the writing top. From underneath the writing top, drill countersunk, 1¼"-deep pilot holes, ⁵⁄₁₆" in from the front edge. Use a piece of tape on your drill bit as a depth guide, making sure you don't drill through the face of the molding. Drive #6 × 1" brass wood screws through the pilot holes and into the molding. Remove the clamps.

MAKE THE TOP PROTECTOR. Cut the top protector (O) to size from ⅛"-thick clear acrylic. Acrylic sheets can be cut with a knife. Using a board or other straightedge as a guide allows you to make repeated cuts to score the material deeply **(photo G).** Then use light pressure to bend and break the material along the score line, leaving the straightedge in position next to the line. Remove the screws holding the front top molding piece, and insert the top protector into the frame.

APPLY FINISHING TOUCHES. Glue and insert ⅜"-dia. oak plugs into all the counterbored holes. Fill all nail holes with wood putty. Sand all the surfaces smooth, and finish the project. We used three coats of clear tung oil to preserve the natural wood tones. Attach 1½ × 3" narrow butt hinges to the top edge of the writing top, and fasten it to the desk top. Because the worksurface is fairly heavy, you may need to support it from behind as you fasten the hinges. To support the worksurface, fasten a 6" heavy-duty lid support near the top of the worksurface and one desk side, inside the storage compartment.

Attach the worksurface to the beveled edge of the desk top with evenly spaced hinges.

Sideboard

This elegant sideboard has plenty of room to hold everything from a meal with all the trimmings to a stack of important files.

The sideboard is an attractive, multipurpose fixture that can be used as a food serving counter, file holder—anything that requires shelf or counter space. The sideboard is a traditional home fixture, adding low-profile storage to just about any area of the home. Positioned against a wall or behind a desk, it does not attract much attention, but, before long, it is the place to go to retrieve an old photo album or game board. Over the years, the sideboard is sure to become a family favorite.

We made the sideboard out of oak and oak plywood. The construction is simple and sturdy. Two long interior shelves span the length of the project, giving you a surprising amount of storage space for such a small unit. The top shelf is covered by two plywood doors, while the bottom shelf is left open for easy access to stored items. Cove molding fastened around the edges of the top and the curved front profiles of the legs add a touch of style to this very simple project.

CONSTRUCTION MATERIALS

Quantity	Lumber
1	¾" × 4 × 8' oak plywood
2	1 × 4" × 8' oak
2	¾ × ¾" × 8' oak cove molding

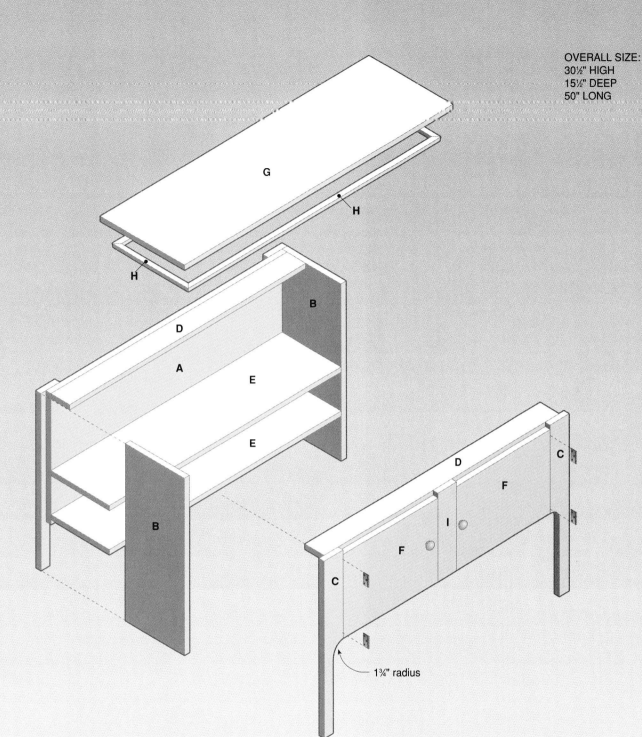

OVERALL SIZE:
30½" HIGH
15½" DEEP
50" LONG

1¾" radius

Cutting List

Key	Part	Dimension	Pcs.	Material
A	Back panel	¾ × 20 × 44"	1	Plywood
B	End panel	¾ × 11 × 29¾"	2	Plywood
C	Leg	¾ × 3½ × 29¾"	4	Oak
D	Cleat	¾ × 2½ × 44"	2	Plywood
E	Shelf	¾ × 10¼ × 44"	2	Plywood

Cutting List

Key	Part	Dimension	Pcs.	Material
F	Door	¾ × 13⅛ × 17⅜"	2	Plywood
G	Top panel	¾ × 15½ × 50"	1	Plywood
H	Top trim	¾ × ¾ × *"	4	Cove molding
I	Stile	¾ × 3½ × 14"	1	Oak

Materials: Brass wood screws (#6 × 2", #6 × 1¼"), brads (1¼"), wood glue, ¾" oak veneer edge tape (35'), 1½ × 3" butt hinges (4), ⅞"-dia. tack-on glides, 1"-dia. brass knobs (2), roller catches (2), finishing materials.

Note: Measurements reflect the actual thickness of dimensional lumber.
*Cut to fit.

Directions: Sideboard

MAKE THE CARCASE. The carcase for the sideboard is the basic cabinet formed by the back, end and top panels. Start by cutting the back panel (A) end panels (B) and shelves (E) from ¾"-thick plywood. We used oak plywood. Use a household iron to apply oak veneer edge tape to one long edge of each shelf. Trim the edges with a utility knife. Sand all the parts smooth, and set the back flat on your worksur-

Support the top shelf with 5¼" spacer blocks on the bottom shelf before fastening it.

face. Position one face of an end panel against each short edge of the back panel. With the top edges flush, mark and drill pilot holes through the end panel and into the back. Use glue and #6 × 2" brass wood screws to attach the back panel between the end panels, keeping the top edges flush. Position the shelves between the end panels, making sure the edge with the veneer tape is facing away from the back panel. Position the bottom face of the bottom shelf flush with the bottom edge of the back. The top shelf should be 5¼" up from the lower shelf. Attach the bottom shelf with glue and #6 × 2" wood screws, driven through the end panels and into the shelves. Set the carcase upright, and position 5¼"-wide spacer blocks on the bottom shelf. Set the top shelf on the spacer blocks. Attach the top shelf with glue and wood screws **(photo A).** Cut the cleats (D) to size. After sanding them smooth, use glue and wood screws to fasten one cleat between the end panels so one long edge is flush with

the front edges of the end panels. Position the remaining cleat with one long edge squarely against the back panel, and fasten the cleat with glue and wood screws.

MAKE THE LEGS. The legs for the sideboard are cut from 1 × 4" oak. They feature curves near the top, tapering downward to 1¾" in width. Cut the legs (C) to length. Designate a top and bottom of each leg. To draw cutting lines, first draw a centerline from top to bottom on each leg. Then, draw reference lines across the legs, 14" and 15¾" up from the bottom. Set a compass to draw a 1¾"-radius semicircle, and position it on the lower reference line. The point of the compass should be on the reference line, as close to an edge as possible. Draw the semicircle to complete the curved portion of the cutting line. Clamp the legs to your worksurface, and use a jig saw to cut the legs to shape, starting at the bottom and following the centerline and semicircle all the way to the end of the top reference line **(photo B).** Sand the legs smooth.

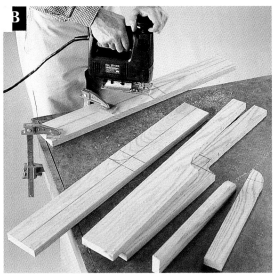

Cut the curved tapers in the legs with a jig saw.

Fasten the legs to the front edges of the end panels. Make sure the outside edges of the legs overhang the end panels by ¼".

Measure the front and back overhang to make sure the top panel is centered on the carcase.

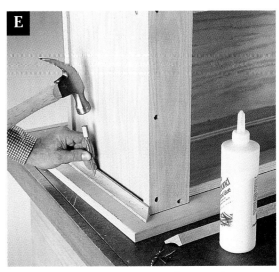

Miter-cut cove molding to cover the seam between the top and the carcase.

ATTACH THE LEGS & STILE. Position two legs against the front edges of the end panels. The cutout sections of the legs should be the inside edges of the legs. Make sure the legs are flush with the end panels at the top and bottom edges, and that they overhang the end panels by ¼". Drill pilot holes, and attach the legs to the ends and shelves with glue and #6 × 2" wood screws **(photo C).** Cut the stile (I) to length. Place it between the legs so it spans the gap between the cleat and top shelf. Center the stile between the legs. Make sure the bottom edge of the stile is flush with the bottom of the top shelf, and attach it with glue and wood screws. Turn the project over, and fasten the remaining legs to the back and ends. Keep the top and bottom edges flush.

INSTALL THE TOP PANEL. Begin by cutting the top panel (G) to size. Apply veneer edge tape to all four edges of the top, and sand the surfaces smooth. Lay the top on a flat surface with its better face facing down. Center the carcase over the top. The top should extend 1½" beyond

the front and back of the carcase **(photo D),** and 2" beyond the outside faces of the end panels. Fasten by driving countersunk, #6 × 1¼" wood screws through the cleats and into the top. Cut the top trim (H) to fit around the underside of the top, miter-cutting the ends at 45° angles so they fit together at the corners. The top edges of the trim pieces should be flush with the edges of the top panel. Attach the top trim with glue and 1¼" brads, driven through the top trim and into the top edges of the top panel. Set the brads with a nail set **(photo E).**

ATTACH THE DOORS. Cut the doors (F) to size. We cut the doors so the grain runs in an opposite, contrasting direction from the carcase. Apply oak veneer edge tape to all four edges of each door. Attach 1½ × 3" brass butt hinges to one short edge of each door, starting 2" in from the tops and from the bottoms. Mount the doors on the carcase by attaching the hinges to the legs. Make sure the bottom edges of the doors are flush with the bottom of the top shelf.

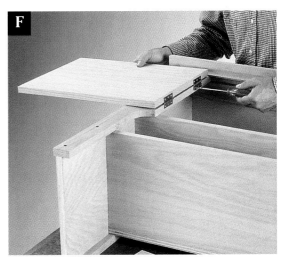

Attach each door to a leg, using 1½ × 3" butt hinges.

APPLY FINISHING TOUCHES. Fill all brad holes with untinted, stainable wood putty. Glue ⅜"-dia. oak plugs into all counterbored screw holes. Finish-sand all the surfaces smooth, remove the door hinges and apply your finish of choice—we used two coats of clear polyurethane. When the finish has dried, reattach the doors. Fasten 1"-dia. brass knobs to the door fronts, and mount roller catches on the doors and stile, 5" down from the top of the stile. Tack furniture glides to the leg bottoms.

Library Ladder

Self-standing, safe and stable, this oak stepladder is truly a top-shelf furnishing.

PROJECT
POWER TOOLS

Floor-to-ceiling bookcases will cease to be unreachable and changing light bulbs in your ceiling fixtures will be less threatening once you've built this charming library ladder. Offering all the safety and convenience of a stepladder, this three-step, rung-style ladder surpasses just about any store-bought climbing structure in style and design. When extended, the runged stepladder sides pro-vide sturdy support for the ladder treads. When not in use, the ladder folds together so it can be stored up against a wall and out of the traffic flow.

Designed for efficiency in use and in construction, this oak stepladder can be built with only three 8'-long 1 × 4 boards and a few feet of oak doweling. The treads are fastened to the sides of the ladder with oak through dowels for long-lasting joints that stand up to repeated use.

SAFETY NOTICE: When using any ladder, always exercise good judgment and safety practices. Make sure the legs of the ladder are firmly planted on a level floor before use. Do not use the dowel rungs as steps. Do not carry heavy objects while using the ladder. This ladder is suitable for light-duty, indoor use only.

CONSTRUCTION MATERIALS

Quantity	Lumber
3	1 × 4" × 8' red oak
2	1"-dia. × 4' oak dowel
1	⅜"-dia. × 4' oak dowel

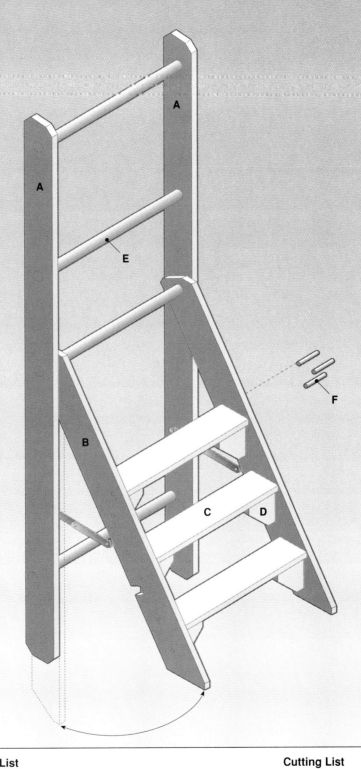

OVERALL SIZE:
58½" HIGH
19⅝" WIDE
25¼" DEEP

A

A

E

B

F

C   D

Cutting List

Key	Part	Dimension	Pcs.	Material
A	Ladder side	¾ × 3½ × 58½"	2	Red oak
B	Step rail	¾ × 3½ × 40¼"	2	Red oak
C	Step tread	¾ × 3½ × 15½"	3	Red oak

Cutting List

Key	Part	Dimension	Pcs.	Material
D	Tread brace	¾ × 3½ × 3½"	6	Red oak
E	Cross dowel	1"-dia. × 19⅜"	4	Oak dowel
F	Through dowel	⅜"-dia. × 2"	18	Oak dowel

Materials: 4d finish nails, wood glue, 10" chest lid supports (2), finishing materials.

Note: Measurements reflect the actual thickness of dimensional lumber.

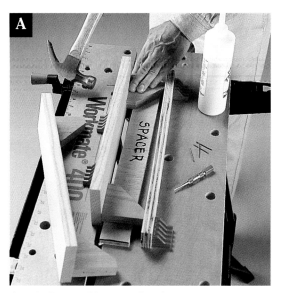

Attach the tread braces ¾" in from the ends of the step rails.

Draw reference lines for positioning the treads parallel to the bottoms of the step rails.

Directions: Library Ladder

MAKE THE LADDER STEPS. The steps for the library ladder consist of flat treads with triangular braces on each end. They are assembled first, then attached to the ladder sides with oak through dowels. Cut the step treads (C) to length from 1 × 4 oak, then cut the tread braces (D) to 3½" square. Mark points 2½" in from one of the corners of each tread brace, then connect the points to make cutting lines. For maximum brace strength, mark the cutting lines so the wood grain in each brace runs vertically when the brace is installed. Make the cutoffs with a jig saw or miter saw, then sand the edges smooth. Attach a brace to each end of each tread **(photo A),** so the outer face of each brace is recessed ½" from the front edge of the tread—use glue and 4d finish nails driven through pilot holes to attach the treads.

MAKE THE STEP RAILS. The step rails support the ladder treads. They are trimmed at one end so they lie flat on the floor when the ladder is set up. Each rail also contains a U-shaped cutout to fit over the bottom rung on the ladder sides. Cut the step rails (B) to length from 1 × 4 red oak. Mark points ¾" in from each corner on one end of each rail, then connect the points to make cutting lines for the triangular cutoffs at the top ends of the rails. Make the cutoffs with a jig saw. On the square end of one rail (this will be the bottom), mark points ⅝" in from one corner, in each direction. Mark another point on the edge, 2" up from the opposite corner. Connect the 2" point to the mark on the bottom to make a 35° cutoff line, then cut with a jig saw or miter saw. Sand the cut smooth, then use the first rail as a template for tracing a matching cutoff onto the other rail— this helps ensure that the legs will be uniform in shape. Cut and sand the second cutoff. Now, mark reference lines for positioning the tread assemblies onto the rails. Measuring up from the bottom, mark points on the shorter edge of each rail at 7½", 15½" and 21½". Set a T-bevel (if you have one) to match the angle on the bottoms of the rails, then use the T-bevel to extend reference lines out from the reference points on the rails—the reference lines should be parallel to the bottoms of the rails **(photo B).** If you don't own a T-bevel, set a 1 × 4 scrap onto one of the rails so the edges are flush and the scrap extends slightly past the bottom end. Trace the bottom cut onto the scrap, extending the line so it runs straight across the scrap board. Cut along the cutting line, then use the 1 × 4 as a guide for tracing the correct angle onto the rails.

ASSEMBLE THE TREADS & RAILS. Attach the tread assemblies between the rails, at the reference lines, using glue and clamps. The fronts of the treads should be flush with the front edges of the rails, with the tops flush up against the reference lines on the rails. When the glue has dried, carefully unclamp the assembly, then drill

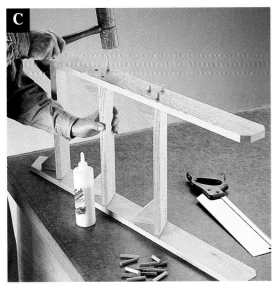

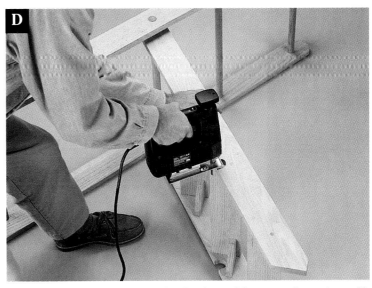

Drive three glued, 2"-long dowels into each step tread joint after the glue in the joints has set.

Cut U-shaped notches into the back edges of the step rails so they will lock over the bottom dowel rung.

three ⅜"-dia. × 1½"-deep dowel holes through the rails and into the tread assemblies at each joint—two of the holes should extend into the end of the tread, and one should extend into the brace. Cut eighteen 2"-long dowel rods from ⅜"-dia. oak doweling (or use ⅜"-dia. dowel pins). Make sure the guide holes are free of sawdust, then apply glue to the ends of each dowel, and insert them into the dowel holes. Drive the dowels all the way into the dowel holes with a wooden mallet, being careful not to break the glue bonds at the joints **(photo C)**. Use a saw to trim the ends of the dowels so they are nearly flush with the rails, then sand the ends flush.

MAKE THE LADDER SIDES. Cut the ladder sides (A) to length. Mark and cut triangular cutoffs with ¾" legs at each corner of each end. Drill 1"-dia. holes through the sides at points centered (edge to edge) at 31", 41½" and 55½" up from the bottoms of the sides. Mark another centerpoint 1¼" in from the back edge of each side, 7½" up

from each bottom. To ensure that these 1"-dia. guide holes for the ladder rungs are aligned, clamp the sides together with all edges and ends flush, and drill through both boards at the same time.

JOIN THE RAILS & LADDER SIDES. The rail/tread assembly is attached to the ladder sides with a 1"-dia. dowel rung that passes through the tops of the rails and is seated in the lowest centered holes in the ladder sides. Drill 1⅛"-dia. guide holes at the top of each step rail, centered from edge to edge and with centerpoints that are 1½" down from the top ends. Set the step assembly between the ladder sides so the holes are aligned with the lowest centered hole in each ladder side. Drive a 1" dowel through all four holes, then slip the ends of the dowel out of the sides in turn, apply glue inside the guide holes in the sides, then reinsert the ends of the dowel. Drill pilot holes, then drive a 4d finish nail through an edge of each ladder side and into the ends of the dowel (this keeps

the dowel from spinning). Also install 1"-dia. dowels in the top two holes. Position the ladder so the rails are flush with the edges of the ladder sides, and trace the lowest holes in the sides onto the outer faces of the rails. Swing the ladder and sides apart, then drill 1¼"-dia. holes through the rails. Draw lines perpendicular to the back edges of the rails, connected to the top and bottom of the hole in each rail. Cut along the lines with a jig saw to make the notches **(photo D)** so the rails will lock over the bottom rung when closed. Install a 1" dowel in the bottom holes in the ladder sides. Install a chest lid support about midway up from the bottom of each rail, then attach the free ends to the ladder sides so the lid support locks into position when the ladder is set up (make sure the ends of the rails and sides all are flush against the floor). Finish-sand the exposed surfaces, then apply your finish of choice—we left the wood uncolored, and applied three coats of water-based polyurethane.

Poker Table

A removable top converts this conventional game table into a custom poker table.

CONSTRUCTION MATERIALS

Quantity	Lumber
1	¾" × 4 × 8' birch plywood
4	1 × 4" × 8' oak
2	1 × 4" × 8' pine
2	1 × 6" × 6' oak
2	2 × 2" × 6' pine
2	⅜ × 1⅛" × 7' oak stop molding
2	¼ × ¾" × 7' pine shelf nosing

The top of this table is designed especially for poker, with an eight-sided playing surface and trays to hold the chips. But for those times when you just need a simple card or game table, the poker tabletop pulls off to create a small four-sided table.

Each leg pulls out easily for storage, but is held securely in place by carriage bolts and wing nuts. With the oak legs and heavy-duty construction, you can play the game without worrying about an untimely collapse—this is no flimsy, fold-down card table. The exterior components are made from oak, while the interior framework and tabletops are made from pine and oak plywood.

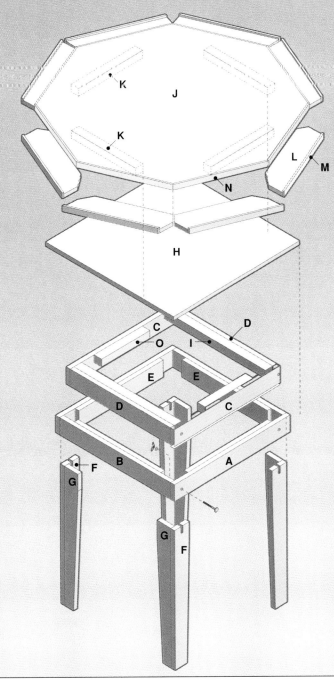

Cutting List

Key	Part	Dimension	Pcs.	Material
A	Apron side	¾ × 3½ × 30"	2	Oak
B	Apron end	¾ × 3½ × 28½"	2	Oak
C	Liner side	¾ × 3½ × 27"	2	Pine
D	Liner end	¾ × 3½ × 25½"	2	Pine
E	Filler block	¾ × 3½ × 21½"	4	Pine
F	Leg front	¾ × 3½ × 30"	4	Oak
G	Leg side	¾ × 2¾ × 30"	4	Oak
H	Main top	¾ × 32 × 32"	1	Plywood

Cutting List

Key	Part	Dimension	Pcs.	Material
I	Main cleat	1½ × 1½ × 19"	2	Pine
J	Poker top	¾ × 48 × 48"	1	Plywood
K	Poker cleat	1½ × 1½ × 16"	4	Pine
L	Tray	¾ × 5½ × 18"	8	Oak
M	Tray trim	¾ × 1¹⁄₁₆ × 18"	8	Stop molding
N	Poker trim	¼ × ¾ × *"	8	Shelf nosing
O	Short cleat	1½ × 1½ × 9"	2	Pine

Materials: Wood screws (#6 × 1¼", #6 × 2", #6 × 2½"), 1¼" brads, wood glue, ¾"-dia. × 3"-long carriage bolts with washers and wing nuts (4), ¾" birch veneer edge tape (15'), finishing materials.
Note: Measurements reflect the actual thickness of dimensional lumber. *Cut to fit.

Use a straightedge guide and scrap-plywood stop blocks when cutting leg tapers with a circular saw.

Position the liner assembly inside the apron assembly so it fits against the filler blocks.

Directions: Poker Table

MAKE THE LEGS. The table legs are designed for heavy-duty support. They are tapered from the top to the bottom. Each leg is made from two 1 × 4 boards butted together. Start by cutting the leg fronts (F) and leg sides (G) to length from 1 × 4" oak. Before cutting the tapers on the leg fronts and leg sides, draw accurate cutting lines. First, designate a top and bottom to each workpiece. Mark a point on the bottoms of the leg fronts, ½" in from one long edge, then draw a mark 3½" down from the tops of the leg fronts on the same long edge. Draw a cutting line connecting the two points on the leg fronts. The leg sides are more narrow than the leg fronts. To draw the cutting lines on the leg sides, mark a point on the bottom of each leg side, 1¼" in from one long edge. Measure and mark a point 3½" down from the top and ¾" in from the same long edge. Draw cutting lines connecting the two points on the leg sides. Use a circular saw with a straight-edge guide to cut along the cutting lines **(photo A).** Support the leg fronts and leg sides with a piece of scrap plywood as you cut them to size. Edge guides made from scrap and stop blocks screwed down at the ends and sides of the workpieces keep the leg parts steady as you cut them. For most ac-curate results, start the taper cuts at the bottom ends. Once the leg sides and leg fronts are cut to shape, butt the unta-pered edges of the leg sides against the leg fronts. With the leg fronts and leg sides flush, drill evenly spaced, counter-bored pilot holes through the leg fronts. Fasten the parts with

Hold the legs firmly, and drill ⅜"-dia. holes through the apron, legs and liner for carriage bolts at all corners.

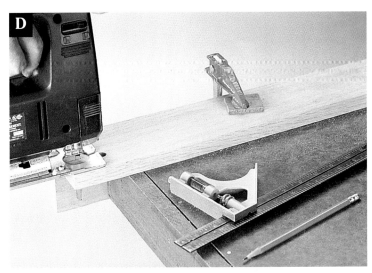

Cut a notch from the top of the leg fronts down to the carriage bolt hole to make it easier to remove and install the legs.

TIP

Apply paste wax over an oil finish for an attractive shine that helps protect the wood. Apply wax in thin coats, then buff thoroughly with a soft rag or chamois before each coat dries completely. For best results, allow at least one full day between buffing the first coat and applying the second coat.

glue and #6 × 1⅝" wood screws, driven through the leg fronts and into the leg sides. Fill all counterbored screw holes with ⅜"-dia. flat wood plugs. Sand the legs smooth.

MAKE THE APRON. The apron is a frame that holds the legs securely at the corners and supports the tabletops. The apron is actually a frame within a frame, made from strong, solid oak on the outside with a less expensive pine liner and filler blocks. L-shaped gaps at the corners of the apron hold the legs, which are secured with carriage bolts and wing nuts. Start by cutting the apron sides (A) and apron ends (B) to size.

Position the apron ends between the apron sides with the the outside faces of the apron ends flush with the ends of the apron sides. Drill counterbored pilot holes, and use glue and #6 × 1⅝" wood screws to fasten the parts. Cut the liner sides (C) and liner ends (D) to size from 1 × 4" pine. Position the liner ends between the liner sides, making sure the edges are flush. Drill pilot holes, and fasten the liner ends between the liner sides with glue and #6 × 2" wood screws, driven through the liner and into the apron. Draw reference lines on the inside faces of the apron sides and apron ends, 3½" in from each corner. Cut the filler blocks (E) to size, and fasten them between the reference lines, using glue and countersunk #6 × 1¼" wood screws. With the apron on a flat surface, set the liner assembly inside the apron **(photo B),** and fasten the liner assembly to the filler blocks with glue and #6 × 2" wood screws.

ATTACH THE LEGS. The legs are inserted into the gaps at the corners of the frame, and secured with carriage bolts. Start by sliding the wide ends of the legs into the gaps at each corner of the apron frame. They should fit snugly, with their tops flush with the apron top. Mark the outside faces of the apron sides for carriage-bolt holes.

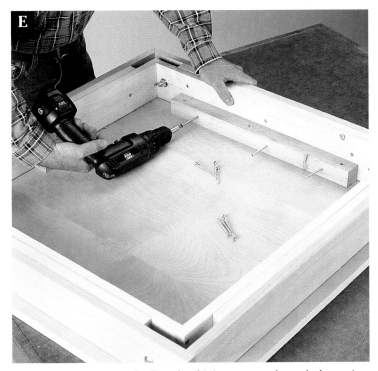

Fasten the main top to the liner by driving screws through the main cleats and short cleats and into the liner and filler blocks.

Center the holes 3¼" in from the apron side ends. With the legs held firmly in place, drill a ⅜"-dia. hole through the apron, legs and liner at each corner **(photo C).** Remove the legs. At the top of the leg fronts, use a jig saw to extend the holes all the way to the top of the leg fronts **(photo D).** These notches allow you to remove the legs for storage without having to remove the carriage bolts. Insert the legs, and push the carriage bolts through the holes. Slide washers on the bolts, and attach wing nuts to secure the legs in place. If one or two legs do not fit precisely, try switching them around—you may find a better fit.

MAKE THE MAIN TOP. The main top is used as a game table and as a base for the poker tabletop. Begin by cutting the main top (H), main cleats (I) and short cleats (O) to size. Sand the parts smooth, and use a household iron to apply self-adhesive birch veneer edge tape to all four edges of the main top. Trim and sand the excess edge tape. Draw reference lines on one face of the main top, 2¼" in from each edge. Center the main cleats and short cleats on the main top with their outside edges on the reference lines. Fasten the cleats, making sure the main cleats are on opposite sides. Test-fit the main top on the apron. If the main top doesn't fit, realign the cleats. Fasten the main top to

Carefully draw the cutting lines for the poker top, using a straight-edge and a homemade compass.

the liner by driving 2½" countersunk screws through the main cleats and into the liner and filler blocks **(photo E).**

MAKE THE POKER TOP. The poker top is a large octagonal tabletop with ledges to hold poker chips. Cleats are attached on the bottom of the poker top so it can be centered over the main top. To cut the poker top (J) to size, start with a 48" square piece of plywood. Marking the octagonal cutting lines requires a little basic geometry. First, draw reference lines between opposite corners, locating the center of the workpiece. Mark the centers of the edges on each of the four sides. Draw lines across the poker top, connecting opposing-edge centerpoints. Next, construct a homemade bar compass by drilling a centered screw hole at one end of a 1 × 2" piece of scrap. (The scrap piece must be at least 25" in

length.) Drill another centered hole for a pencil, 24" up from the first hole. Drive a screw through the first hole and into the poker top center point. Slip a pencil into the remaining hole, and rotate the bar compass to draw a 48"-dia. circle on the poker top. Using a straightedge, draw cutting lines connecting the points where the reference lines intersect with the circle **(photo F).** Cut along the cutting lines with a circular saw, and sand the poker top to smooth out any rough edges or saw marks. To cut the poker trim (N) to fit against the poker top sides, use a power miter box or a backsaw and miter box to cut a 22½° outside bevel at one end of a poker trim piece. NOTE: 22½° is commonly marked on miter boxes, circular saws and radial-arm saws. After cutting

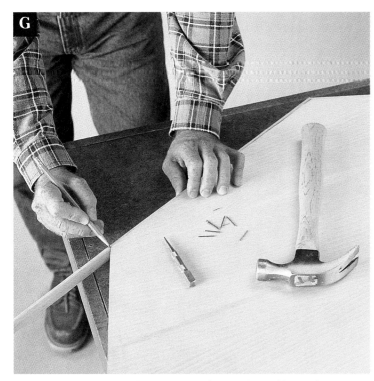

Mark the trim pieces to fit the edges of the poker table, and cut them to length with a 22½° bevel.

this bevel, position the poker trim against one edge of the poker top. Mark the trim where the next point contacts it **(photo G),** then cut another bevel that slants in the opposite direction from the bevel at the other end. Attach the trim piece to the poker top with glue and 1¼" brads, and continue cutting and measuring the poker trim to fit the table. Fill all the brad holes with wood putty, and sand the edges smooth when dry.

ATTACH THE TRAYS. Trays are attached to each edge of the octagonal poker top to hold poker chips. Cut the trays (L) and tray trim (M) to size. In order for the trays to fit on the underside of the poker top, the inside corners on one long edge on each tray are trimmed off at a 45° angle. Draw cutting lines at each end of one long edge, forming a triangle with 2"-long sides, and use a power miter box or a circular saw to cut the corners. Use glue and 1¼" brads to fasten the tray trim to the square long edge of each tray so the bottoms are flush. Turn the poker top upside down. Use glue and #6 × 1¼" wood screws to fasten the trays to the poker top at each straight edge. The trays should extend 3½" beyond the poker top edges, so use a piece of 1 × 4 as a spacer between the tray trim and the poker top edges as you fit the pieces together. Cut the poker cleats (K) to size, and position them on the poker top centerlines. (The poker cleats hold the poker top in place while it sits on the main top.) Center the poker cleats on the lines, and make sure their inside edges are 16⅛" in from the center of the table. Fasten the poker cleats with glue and #6 × 1¼" wood screws **(photo H).**

APPLY FINISHING TOUCHES. Set all nail heads and fill all nail holes with untinted, stainable wood putty. Glue ⅜"-dia. oak plugs into all screw counterbores, then sand to level. Finish-sand all surfaces, and apply your finish of choice. We used three coats of tung oil.

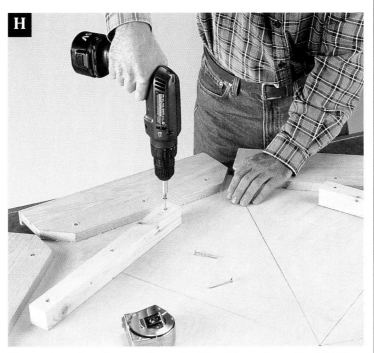

Fasten the poker cleats to the underside of the poker table, 16⅛" in from the centers.

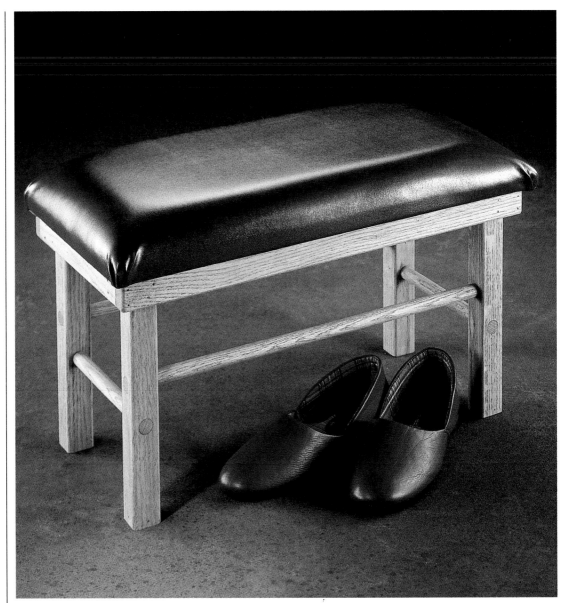

Oak Footstool

*Rugged simplicity is the hallmark of this versatile
and easy-to-build oak footstool.*

CONSTRUCTION MATERIALS

Quantity	Lumber
1	2 × 2" × 8' red oak
1	1 × 2" × 6' red oak
1	¾" × 2 × 4' plywood
2	¾"-dia. × 3' oak dowels

This simple footstool features rugged construction and adaptable styling so it can blend into nearly any den or family room. Select an upholstery style that works with your decor, and this footstool will look as if it was custom-made just for your room.

The support framework is made of solid red oak, with oak through-dowel stringers that give it a subtle design touch.

Call it a footstool, an ottoman or even a hassock. Use it to rest and elevate your tired feet, or employ it as extra seating in front of your television. Whatever you call it and however you use it, this oak footstool will quickly become one of your most useful furnishings.

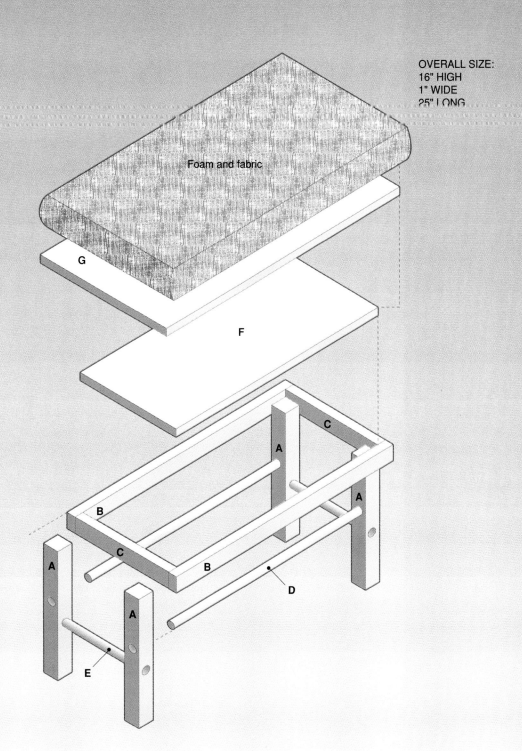

OVERALL SIZE:
16" HIGH
1" WIDE
25" LONG

Foam and fabric

G

F

A

C

A

B

C

B

D

A

A

E

Key	Part	Dimension	Pcs.	Material
A	Leg	1½ × 1½ × 12"	4	Red oak
B	Apron	¾ × 1½ × 24"	2	Red oak
C	Apron	¾ × 1½ × 10½"	2	Red oak
D	Stringer	¾"-dia. × 22½"	2	Oak dowel

Key	Part	Dimension	Pcs.	Material
E	Stringer	¾"-dia. × 10½"	2	Oak dowel
F	Top	¾ × 10½ × 22½"	1	Plywood
G	Seat board	¾ × 13 × 25"	1	Plywood

Cutting List (×2)

Materials: 6d brass-plate finish nails, #6 × 1¼" brass wood screws, 2 × 13 × 25" high-density foam rubber, 19 × 31" upholstery fabric, upholstery tacks, rubber glides or tack-on chair glides (4), finishing materials.

Note: Measurements reflect the actual thickness of dimensional lumber.

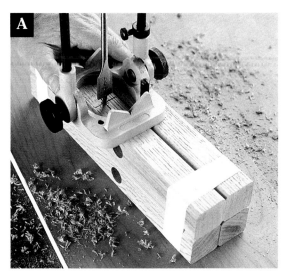

With the legs taped in a square bundle, use a drill and a portable drill guide to make the dowel holes.

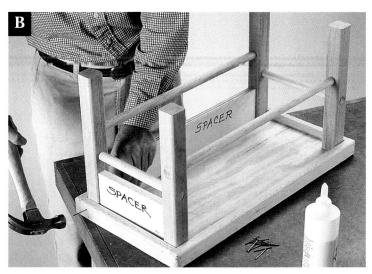

Position spacers between the legs for support, and attach the apron to the leg assembly.

Directions: Oak Footstool

MAKE THE LEGS. All four legs for the footstool can be cut from one 8'-long oak 2 × 2. Before you cut the individual legs to length, round over the edges of the 8' board with a router and ¼" roundover bit, or with a power sander. Cut the legs (A) to length. Bundle them together edge to edge to form a square, and wrap masking tape around the bundle to hold it together. Mark and drill dowel holes for the through-dowel stringers: on one side, measure in 5" from the ends of the 2 × 2s, and draw a reference line across both exposed faces. Mark drilling points at the center of the reference line on each face. Drill through the drilling point with a ¾" spade bit (set the block on a piece of scrapwood to prevent drill tearout). Use a portable drill guide to make sure the hole is perpendicular **(photo A).** Next, give the bundle of legs a quarter turn, and draw a reference line on the exposed faces 5" in from the other end of the leg bundle. Mark centered drilling

points and drill ¾" dowel holes at each point. Remove the tape from the legs, and sand the drill bit entry and exit points until smooth.

BUILD THE APRONS. The aprons for the footstool are cut from oak 1 × 2, and attached at the tops of the legs to create a ¾"-deep recess for the plywood top. Round over an 8'-long oak 1 × 2, then cut the aprons (B, C) to length. Sand the ends smooth. Cut the top (F) to use as a spacer for attaching the aprons. Set the top on your worksurface, then wrap the top with the apron pieces so the ends of the longer aprons (B) are flush with the outer faces of the shorter aprons (C). Fasten the aprons together with glue and 6d brass-plated finish nails driven through pilot holes at each joint.

BUILD THE LEG ASSEMBLY. The leg assembly is built by attaching the legs with dowel stretchers and then fastening the assembly to the apron. Set the legs on your worksurface, making sure the legs are arranged so the dowel holes are aligned correctly (see *Dia-*

gram, page 33). Cut the stringers (D, E) to length from ¾" oak doweling. Sand the ends smooth. Dry-fit the stringers in the dowel holes. Poke each stringer end back out through each dowel hole an inch or two, then apply wood glue to the end of the stringer. Make sure all stringer ends are glued and flush with the outer faces of the legs, then reinforce each joint by driving 6d finish nails through the legs and into the ends of the stringers. Sand to make sure the dowel ends are flush with the legs. Set the legs on the top board, at the corners of the apron frame. Use spacer blocks cut from scrap to fit exactly between the leg pairs, holding them so they are perpendicular to the apron. Attach the legs to the frame with 6d finish nails and glue **(photo B).**

APPLY THE FINISH. Finish-sand the footstool frame, with 180- or 220-grit sandpaper. Wipe down with mineral spirits, and allow the wood to dry completely. Apply wood coloring agent: we used two coats of rub-on black walnut stain.

Staple the upholstery to the back of the seat board, making sure it is even and taut.

Attach the upholstered top board by driving 1¼" screws up through the seat board.

the good side facing down. Center the seat board (foam-side down) onto the back of the material. Press down lightly and evenly on the board, then pull up one end of the material and tack it to the seat board with a staple gun. Pull up the opposite end, tugging on the material until it is taut. Tack the end **(photo C).** Tuck in the corners, and tack the remaining edges in place the same way. Turn the seat board over and inspect your work. If you aren't happy with it, it's easy to redo it at this point. Once the upholstery is tacked on to your satisfaction, fasten the edges to the seat board with upholstery tacks spaced at 2" intervals.

INSTALL THE SEAT. Set the plywood top (F) into the recess at the top of the apron frame. Drill pilot holes, and attach the top to the legs with #6 × 1⅝" wood screws. Make sure the top of the board is flush with the top of the apron frame. Lay the upholstered seat facedown on a clean, flat worksurface. Invert the leg assembly, and position it over the underside of the seat board. Make sure the overhang is equal on all sides, drill pilot holes, and drive #6 × 1¼" wood screws through the top board and into the seat board around the perimeter of the board **(photo D).**

Apply a topcoat: we used three coats of rub-on tung oil. Tack chair glides to the bottom of each leg.

MAKE THE SEAT. The soft, upholstered footstool seat extends past the edges of the frame slightly. We used dark brown leather upholstery tacked onto the seat board over 2"-thick high-density foam rubber. Choose any style of upholstery that blends with your room furnishings, but make sure to use upholstery fabric. Cut the seat board (G) to size, and sand the edges smooth. Cut the 2"-thick foam rubber to the same dimensions as the seat board. To keep the foam from shifting as you attach the upholstery, tack it to the seat board with double-edge carpet tape or spray-mount adhesive. Cut the upholstery so it is large enough to extend at least 3" past each seat board edge. Lay the material on a clean, flat surface with

TIP

Leather upholstery is a traditional choice for furnishings that reflect the style of this oak footstool. But, if you prefer, you can substitute vinyl upholstery with a leather look. If you are building a footstool for a specific chair, either find upholstery that matches the chair pattern exactly, or use material that complements or contrasts. The most disappointing results occur when you use material that's a near match, but is noticeably different.

Bookcase

A simple, functional bookcase on which to set your picture frames, books and decorations, this project is as useful as it is attractive.

PROJECT POWER TOOLS

A functional, attractive bookcase adds just the right decorative and functional touch to a den or family room. And you don't need to shell out large amounts of cash for a high-end bookcase or settle for a cheap, throw-together particleboard unit—this sturdy bookcase looks great and will last for years.

Four roomy shelf areas let you display and store everything from framed pictures to reference manuals in the bookcase. The decorative trim on the outside of the bookcase spices up the overall appearance of the project, while cove molding along the front edges softens the corners and adds structural stability. With a few coats of enamel paint, this bookcase takes on a smooth, polished look.

Although the project is constructed mostly of plywood, the molding that fits around the top, bottom and shelves allows the bookcase to look great in almost any room of the house. This bookcase is a great-looking, useful project that you will have fun building.

Construction Materials

Quantity	Lumber
1	¾" × 4 × 8' birch plywood
1	¼" × 4 × 8' birch plywood
2	¾ × 1⅝" × 8' panel molding
1	¼ × ¾" × 8' cove molding
2	¾ × 1⅝" × 8' quarter-round molding
1	¾ × 2⅝" × 6' chair-rail molding

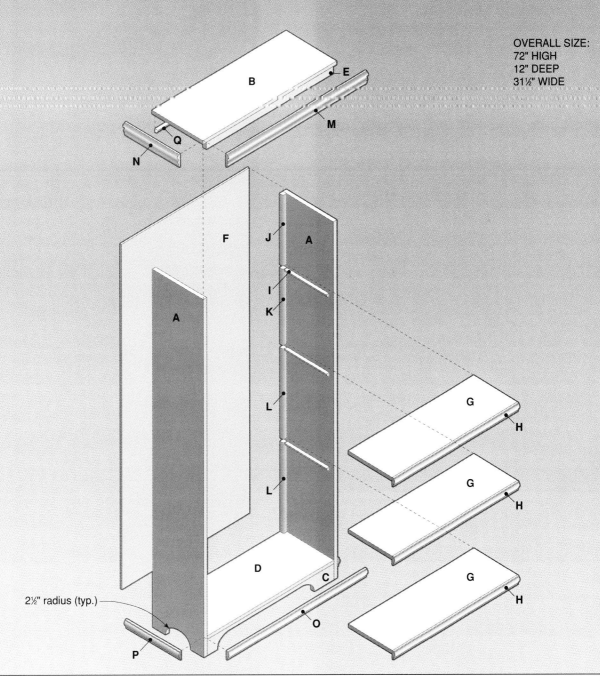

OVERALL SIZE:
72" HIGH
12" DEEP
31½" WIDE

2½" radius (typ.)

Cutting List

Key	Part	Dimension	Pcs.	Material
A	Side	¾ × 12 × 71¼"	2	Plywood
B	Top	¾ × 11¾ × 31½"	1	Plywood
C	Front rail	¾ × 3¼ × 30"	1	Plywood
D	Bottom	¾ × 11¾ × 30"	1	Plywood
E	Top rail	¾ × 1½ × 30"	1	Plywood
F	Back	¼ × 30 × 68¾"	1	Plywood
G	Shelf	¾ × 10½ × 30"	3	Plywood
H	Shelf nosing	¾ × 1⅝ × 30"	3	Panel molding
I	Shelf cleat	¾ × ¾ × 9¾"	6	Cove molding

Cutting List

Key	Part	Dimension	Pcs.	Material
J	Back brace	¾ × ¾ × 14"	2	Quarter-round
K	Back brace	¾ × ¾ × 15"	2	Quarter-round
L	Back brace	¾ × ¾ × 18"	4	Quarter-round
M	Top facing	¾ × 2⅝ × 33"	1	Chair-rail molding
N	Top side molding	¾ × 2⅝ × 12¾"	2	Chair-rail molding
O	Bottom facing	¾ × 1⅝ × 33"	1	Panel molding
P	Bottom side molding	¾ × 1⅝ × 12¾"	2	Panel molding
Q	Back brace	¾ × ¾ × 28½"	1	Quarter-round

Materials: #6 × 2" wood screws, finish nails (4d, 6d), glue, 1¼" brads, ¾" wire nails, ¾" birch veneer edge tape (25'), finishing materials.

Note: Measurements reflect the actual thickness of dimensional lumber.

Directions: Bookcase

MAKE THE SIDES & FRONT RAIL. The bookcase sides and the front rail have arches cut into their bottom edges to create the bookcase "feet." Start by cutting the sides (A) and front rail (C) to size from ¾"-thick plywood. (We used birch plywood.) Sand the parts smooth. Clean the edges thoroughly, then cut strips of ¾" self-adhesive veneer tape slightly longer than the long

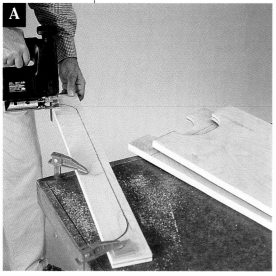

Arches cut along the bottoms of the side panels and front rail create the bookcase "feet."

edges of each side. Attach the tape by positioning it over one long edge of each side, then pressing it with a household iron set at a medium-low setting. The heat will activate the adhesive. Sand the edges and surfaces of the taped edges to smooth out any rough spots. To make the arches in the sides, designate a top and bottom to each side, and draw a cutting line across them, 2½" up from the bottom edge. Draw marks on the bottom edges of the sides, 5½" in from the front and rear edges. Set a compass to draw a 2½"-radius arc, using the marks on the bottom edges as centerpoints: set the point of the compass as close to the bottom edges of the sides as possible, and draw the arcs. Use a jig saw to cut along the lines. Repeat these steps to make the arch in the front rail, but place the point of the compass 4¾" in from each end of the front rail. Cut the front rail to shape with a jig saw **(photo A).**

BUILD THE CARCASE. The top, bottom and sides of the bookcase form the basic cabinet—

called the carcase. Begin by cutting the top (B), bottom (D) and top rail (E) to size. Sand the parts to smooth out any rough edges. Draw reference lines across the faces of the sides, 3¼" up from the bottom edges. Set the sides on edge, and position the bottom between them, just above the reference lines. Attach the bottom to the sides with glue and countersunk #6 × 2" wood screws, leaving a ¼" setback at the back edge. Set the sides upright, and position the front rail between the sides, flush with the side and bottom edges. Glue the rail ends, then clamp it to the bottom board. Drill pilot holes, and secure the front rail with 6d finish nails driven through the sides, and 1¼" brads driven through the bottom **(photo B).** Set all nail heads below the wood surface. Use glue and 6d finish nails to attach the top to the top ends of the sides, keeping the side and front edges flush. Fasten the top rail between the sides, flush with the front edges of the sides and top. Use glue and 6d finish nails to secure the top rail in place.

MAKE THE BACK. Quarter-round molding is attached on the sides and top to serve as retainer strips for the ¼"-thick plywood back. Cut the back braces (J, K, L, Q) to size from quarter-round

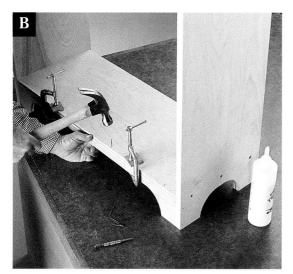

Clamp the front rail to the bottom, and fasten it with glue, finish nails and brads.

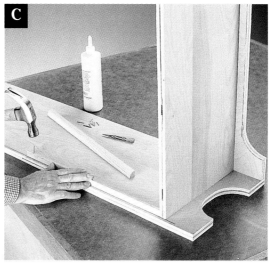

Attach the back braces to the sides, creating a ¼" recess for the back panel.

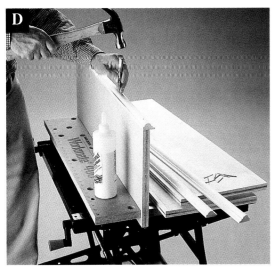

Strips of panel molding are attached to the front edges of the shelves.

Attach the shelf cleats with glue and 1¼" brads.

molding. Set the carcase on its side. Starting at the bottom, use glue and 1¼" brads to fasten the back braces to the sides and top, ¼" in from the back edges **(photo C).** Use a ¾"-thick spacer to create gaps for the shelves between the strips. Position the carcase so it rests on its front edges. Set the back in place so it rests on the back braces, and secure it with tape. Check for square by measuring diagonally from corner to corner across the back. When the measurements are the same, the carcase is square. Drive ¾" wire nails through the back and into the back braces. Do not glue the back in place.

MAKE THE SHELVES. Shelves are cut to size and inserted in the carcase between the back braces. The shelves are supported by cleats. Cut the shelves (G) and shelf nosing (H) to size. Drill pilot holes, and use glue and 4d finish nails to attach the nosing to the shelves, keeping the top edges flush **(photo D).** Set the nail heads. Cut the shelf cleats (I) to size. To help you position the shelf cleats, use a combination square to draw reference lines square to the front edges of each side. Start the lines at the top of the lower back braces (K, L), and extend them to within 1" of the front edges of the sides. Apply glue to the shelf cleats, and position them on the reference lines. Attach the shelf cleats to the inside faces of the sides with 1¼" brads **(photo E).** Apply glue to the top edges of the shelf cleats, then slide the shelves onto the cleats. Drive 6d finish nails through the sides and into the ends of the shelves. Drive ¾" wire nails through the back panel and into the rear edges of the shelves.

APPLY FINISHING TOUCHES. Cut the top facing (M), top side molding (N), bottom facing (O) and bottom side molding (P) to size. Miter-cut both ends of the top facing and bottom facing and the front ends of the side moldings at a 45° angle so the molding pieces will fit together where they meet at the corners. Fasten the molding at the top with glue and 4d finish nails, keeping the top edges flush with the bookcase. Attach the bottom molding, keeping the top edges flush with the bottom. To help you align the bottom side molding, draw reference lines on the sides before attaching the pieces. The reference lines should be flush with the top of the bottom facing **(photo F).** Attach the bottom side molding. Fill all holes with wood putty, and finish-sand the project. Finish as desired—we used primer and two coats of interior enamel paint.

Using a combination square, draw lines on the sides, aligned with the top of the bottom facing.

Library Table

This solid oak library table features a clean, sophisticated appearance that suits any den or study.

CONSTRUCTION MATERIALS

Quantity	Lumber
1	¾" × 4 × 8' oak plywood
1	½ × 12" × 4' oak plywood
2	1 × 2" × 6' oak
3	1 × 4" × 8' oak
2	1 × 6" × 6' oak
2	2 × 2" × 8' oak

High-quality, great-looking furniture doesn't need to be overly expensive or difficult to make, and this library table is the proof. We used a traditional design for this old favorite. The simple drawer construction, beautiful oak materials and slender framework add up to one great-looking table.

Consider the possibilities for this table in your den or study. These areas of the home call out for a simple, yet elegant, table to support a lamp, books or just to add a decorative accent. We applied a two-toned finish, but no matter how you finish it, this library table serves many duties—and it looks great in the process.

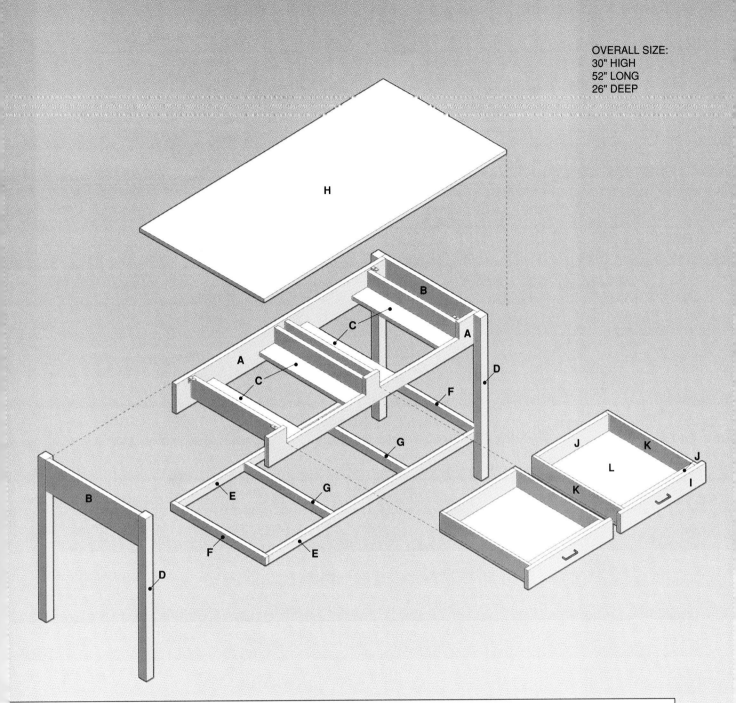

OVERALL SIZE:
30" HIGH
52" LONG
26" DEEP

Cutting List

Key	Part	Dimension	Pcs.	Material
A	Side	¾ × 5½ × 44½"	2	Oak
B	End	¾ × 5½ × 20"	2	Oak
C	Guide	¾ × 3½ × 18½"	8	Oak
D	Leg	1½ × 1½ × 29¼"	4	Oak
E	Side rail	¾ × 1½ × 44½"	2	Oak
F	End rail	¾ × 1½ × 20"	2	Oak

Cutting List

Key	Part	Dimension	Pcs.	Material
G	Cross rail	¾ × 1½ × 18½"	2	Oak
H	Top	¾ × 26 × 52"	1	Plywood
I	Drawer front	¾ × 3½ × 18"	2	Oak
J	Drawer end	¾ × 2⅜ × 15⅞"	4	Oak
K	Drawer side	½ × 2⅜ × 19"	4	Plywood
L	Drawer bottom	½ × 16⅞ × 19"	2	Oak

Materials: Wood screws (#6 × 1¼", #6 × 1⅝", #6 × 2"), 1¼" brads, wood glue, corner brackets (4), ¾" oak veneer edge tape (25'), 4" drawer pulls (2), ⅞"-dia. rubber feet (4), tack-on furniture glides (4), finishing materials.

Note: Measurements reflect the actual thickness of dimensional lumber.

Measure the diagonals, and adjust the apron frame as needed until it is square.

Tape 8"-long blocks of scrapwood to the legs to hold the rail assembly for installation.

Directions: Library Table

MAKE THE APRON ASSEMBLY. The apron section of the library table holds the drawers. It is made by attaching the sides, ends and guides. Start by cutting the sides (A) and ends (B) to size, and sand them smooth. Choose which side you want to be the front, and draw the two 3"-deep × 17"-long rectangular outlines for the drawer cutouts on it. The outlines should start 3¾" in from each end of the front. Use a jig saw and a straightedge guide to make the cutouts. Drill counterbored pilot holes, and attach the sides between the ends with glue and #6 × 1⅝" wood screws, driven through the ends and into the sides. Make sure the outside faces of the sides are flush with the ends. Cut the guides (C) to length. The guides are attached in pairs to form supporting corners on either side of the drawer notches. Fasten the guides together in right-angle pairs: butt one guide's long edge against the

face of another guide, making sure their ends are flush, and attach the guides with glue and wood screws. Position the guide pairs between the sides so the inside faces are flush with the bottom and sides of the rectangular cutouts. (Set the guide pairs on spacers to keep them aligned with the cutouts as you work.) Before fastening the guides, check for square by measuring from corner to corner **(photo A).** If the measurements are not the

same, adjust as needed. Drive 6d finish nails through the sides and into the guides to fasten them in place. Use a nail set to set the nail heads below the surface of the wood.

MAKE THE RAIL ASSEMBLY. The rail assembly is a frame that provides stability to the legs. Start by cutting the side rails (E), end rails (F) and cross rails (G) to size. Position the side rails on edge. Drill counterbored pilot holes, and attach the end rails with glue

Support the drawer with a ½"-thick scrap to center the drawer front correctly. Clamp the front to the drawer before driving screws.

and #6 × 2" wood screws—the resulting rectangular frame should sit flat on your worksurface. Attach the cross rails between the side rails, 14" in from the inside edges of the end rails. Fill all counterbores with ⅜"-dia. wood plugs. Sand the rail assembly smooth.

ASSEMBLE THE TABLE. Begin by cutting the legs (D) to size. Sand the legs to smooth out any rough spots and sharp edges. Use glue and wood screws to fasten the legs to the apron so the top edges and outside faces are flush. Be careful not to drill into the screws connecting the sides and ends. Stand the table up, then clamp or tape 8"-long scrap blocks to the inside edges of the legs, flush with the bottom leg edges. These scrap blocks hold the rail assembly in place as you attach it. Apply glue, and fasten the rail assembly to the legs, making sure the end rails are flush with the outside edges of the legs **(photo B).** Cut the top (H) to size. Clean the edges thoroughly, then cut strips of ¾" self-adhesive veneer edge tape slightly longer than all four

edges of each top. Attach the tape by positioning it over the edges, then pressing it with a household iron set at a medium-low setting. The heat will activate the adhesive. Sand the top, and choose which side of the top you want to face up. Choose the smoothest, most attractive side to face up. Draw reference lines on the underside of the top, 2¼" in from the long edges. Fasten two 2" corner brackets on each line, 2¼" in from the top ends. Attach the top to the apron with screws driven through the corner brackets and into the top and apron.

MAKE THE DRAWERS. Start by cutting the drawer ends (J) and drawer sides (K) to size. Sand them to smooth out any rough spots, and fasten the drawer ends between the drawer sides, using glue and 4d finish nails. Make sure the outside faces of the drawer ends are flush with the ends of the drawer sides, and set all the nails with a nail set. Cut the drawer bottoms (L) to size. Center a bottom over a pair of drawer ends and a pair of drawer sides. Drill pilot holes for 4d finish nails, and attach

the bottom to the drawer ends and sides, driving the nails through the bottom and into the edges. Do not use glue to attach the drawer bottoms. Cut the drawer fronts (I) to size. To attach the drawer fronts, first set the drawers on a ½"-thick piece of scrap. This piece of scrap will make sure the top-to-bottom spacing is correct when you attach the drawer front. Check to make sure there is an equal distance between the ends of the drawer fronts and the drawer sides on both ends of the drawer fronts **(photo C).** Clamp the drawer fronts in place, and fasten the drawer fronts to the drawers with countersunk, #6 × 1¼" wood screws, driven through the drawer ends and into the drawer fronts. Test-fit the drawers in the apron. Adjust the fronts if they are uneven on the front of the apron.

APPLY FINISHING TOUCHES. Fill all screw counterbores with glued oak plugs, and fill all nail holes with wood putty. Finish-sand the entire project with 180-grit sandpaper, and apply your choice of finish. We applied a mahogany-colored stain to the apron and rubbed a natural oil finish on the drawer fronts and top. We also applied three coats of paste wax to the tabletop for extra protection. When the finish has dried, install the drawer pulls on the drawer fronts, and wax the top faces of the guides with paraffin. Insert the drawers, and set the table on its back edges. Attach ⅞"-dia. rubber feet to the bottom of the drawers to prevent them from being pulled out of the table **(photo D).** Attach furniture glides to the leg bottoms.

Slide the drawers into place, then install rubber feet at the back corners to serve as drawer stops and keep the drawers centered.

PROJECT
POWER TOOLS

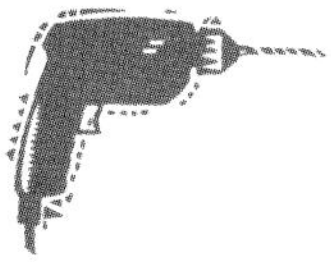

Book Stand

Display a beloved volume for others to enjoy, or hold your text open for hands-free reading.

Construction Materials

Quantity	Lumber
1	¾" × 2 × 4' oak plywood
1	1 × 4" × 3' oak
1	¾ × 1⅝" × 6' oak patio stop
2	⅜ × ¾" × 7' oak shelf nosing

The traditional look of a hardwood book stand has long been a fixture in dens and studies. This sturdy, oak book stand can hold books of all types and sizes at several different angles, making reading easier and more enjoyable. But in addition to the practical uses for book stands, many people prefer to use book stands as decorative accents for displaying favorite antique volumes.

In this book stand design, the gallery-spindle oak pegs on the book ledge keep books open. The ledge can be positioned at a low angle or a high angle with the same degree of stability—whichever is more comfortable for you.

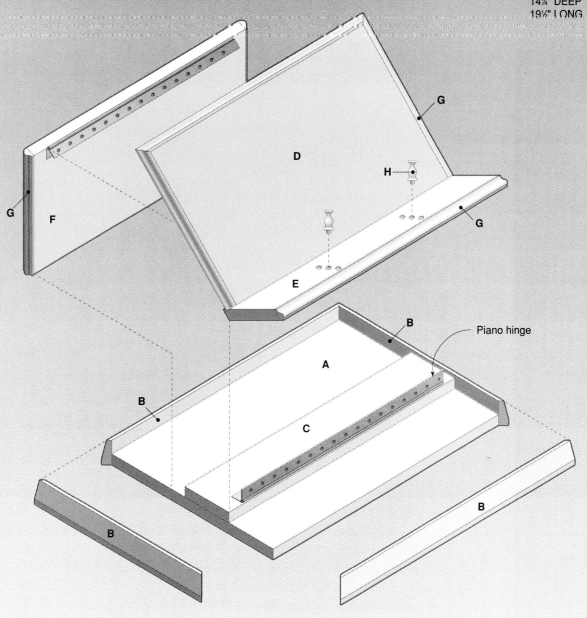

OVERALL SIZE:
15" HIGH
14¼" DEEP
19½" LONG

Piano hinge

Cutting List

Key	Part	Dimension	Pcs.	Material
A	Base board	¾ × 12¾ × 18"	1	Plywood
B	Base molding	¾ × 1¾ × *"	4	Stop molding
C	Step	¾ × 3½ × 18"	1	Oak
D	Book rest	¾ × 12 × 17"	1	Plywood

Cutting List

Key	Part	Dimension	Pcs.	Material
E	Ledge	¾ × 3½ × 17¾"	1	Oak
F	Support	¾ × 8 × 16⅞"	1	Plywood
G	Trim	⅜ × ¾ × *"	6	Shelf nosing
H	Peg	⅝"-dia. × 1¼"	2	Gallery spindles

Materials: Wood screws (#6 × 1¼", #6 × 2"), brads (1", 1¼"), wood glue, 14"-long narrow piano hinges (2), (12 x 18") adhesive-backed felt, finishing materials.

Note: Measurements reflect the actual thickness of dimensional lumber.
*Cut to fit.

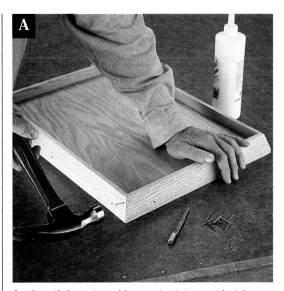

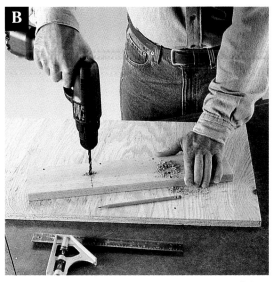

Lock-nail the mitered base trim joints with 4d finish nails.

Draw reference lines on the ledge, and drill ¼"-dia. holes for the pegs along the lines.

Directions: Book Stand

BUILD THE BASE SECTION. The heavy base section is made by framing a piece of oak plywood with oak stop molding. Start by cutting the base (A) to size from ¾"-thick oak plywood, and sand it to smooth out any rough edges. Cut the base molding (B) from stop molding to fit around the edges of the base. Measure the edges of the base carefully, and miter-cut the ends of the base molding at 45° angles to fit together at the corners. Sand all parts after cutting to smooth out any rough spots. To avoid splitting the pieces when you attach them to the base, drill pilot holes for 1¼" brads through the base molding. Glue the molding, and fasten it around the edges of the base. Be sure to glue the ends of the molding, and drive brads through the pieces at the joints, "lock-nailing" the mitered joints **(photo A).** Set the brads with a nail set so they are recessed below the surface of the wood.

MAKE THE STAND SECTION. The stand section supports the book when the book stand is used. All three components (the book rest, ledge and support) have decorative trim attached to one or more edges. The ledge features holes for adjustable pegs (H) that hold the book open. For pegs, we used ⅝"-dia. × 1¼" gallery spindles with a short tenon at one end. Begin by cutting the book rest (D), ledge (E) and support (F) to size. After sanding the parts smooth, draw two reference lines on one face of the ledge, 5½" in from each end. Drill three evenly spaced holes for the pegs on each reference line **(photo B).** (Check the diameter of your pegs before drilling the holes.) We drilled the peg holes ¼", 1" and 1¾" in from the front edge of the ledge. Cut the trim (G) from shelf nosing to fit onto the front edge of the ledge. The ends of the ledge trim should be square and flush with the ends of the ledge. Fasten the ledge trim to the front edge of the ledge, using glue and 1¼" brads.

Cut the trim (G) from shelf nosing to fit around three edges of the book rest, miter-cutting the top corners at 45° angles. Attach the trim with glue and 1¼" brads. Also cut and attach trim to the short edges of the support. Set the brads with a nail set, and sand the trim smooth.

ATTACH THE LEDGE & BOOK REST. The ledge and book rest are attached to form a right-angle assembly that can support a large book. Set the book rest flat on your worksurface with the square, long edge of the ledge down. Butt the top face of the ledge against the untrimmed edge of the book rest, forming a right-angle assembly. Drill pilot holes, and attach the ledge to the book rest with glue and #6 × 1⅝" wood screws, driven through the ledge and into the book rest. Stand the assembly up, and test-fit the pegs in the ledger holes **(photo C).** When test-fitting, make sure there is a little extra play to allow for the finishing products that will be applied to the pegs and the holes.

Test-fit the pegs into the holes in the ledge. If the fit is tight, trim the tenons with a file.

ATTACH THE SUPPORT & STEP. When assembled, the book stand can support a book at two different angles. Position the support against the back face of the book rest, with the side edges flush. The bottom edge of the support should rest squarely on your worksurface. Draw a reference line on the book rest to mark the top edge of the support. This reference line will help you position the parts when you attach them. Next, cut the step (C) to size. The step anchors the book rest and ledge to the base. Sand the step smooth, and test-fit it on the base, making sure it fits between the base molding pieces. Remove the step from the base. Center a 14"-long piano hinge against the rear edge of the ledge, and attach it. Attach the remaining hinge leaf to the step so the barrel just reaches one long edge of the step. Position a ¾"-thick piece of scrap under the ledge as you fasten the hinge, raising the book rest to the proper height. Attach a 14"-long piano hinge to the back face of the book rest, keeping the barrel of the hinge flush with the reference line. Lay the book rest face down, and attach the remaining hinge leaf to the inside face of the support, making sure the support is centered on the book rest. Draw a reference line on the top of the base, 3½" in from the inside edge of the front base molding. Apply glue to the step, and set the book rest assembly onto the base so the front edge of the step is flush with the reference line. Push the support forward as far as it can go. The bottom edge of the support should rest on the step. Drill pilot holes, and attach the step to the base with two #6 × 1¼" wood screws **(photo D).**

APPLY FINISHING TOUCHES. Begin by filling all the nail holes with wood putty. Sand the project smooth, and stain and finish the book stand as desired. We used a dark stain and a tung oil topcoat. To avoid gumming up the piano hinges with finishing materials, cover the hinges with masking tape. When the finish has dried, remove the tape. Apply adhesive-backed glides or strips of adhesive-backed felt to the bottom of the book stand to prevent scratching on tabletops.

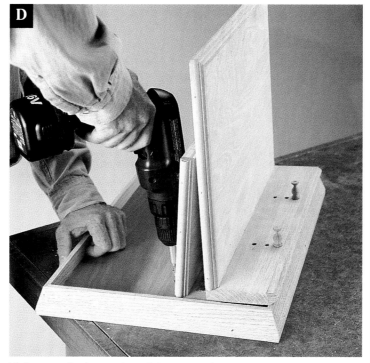

Make sure the front edge of the step is flush with the reference line drawn on the base, then fasten it with glue and screws.

Blanket Chest

*This traditional blanket chest is also just the right
size to serve as a coffee table.*

CONSTRUCTION MATERIALS

Quantity	Lumber
1	¾" × 4 × 8' plywood
1	½ × 1⅜" × 7' stop molding
1	¼ × 1⁵⁄₁₆" × 7' corner molding
2	¾ × 1⅜" × 7' shelf cap

This roomy blanket chest makes the most of valuable floor space in your den or family room. Large enough to hold several blankets, sheets and afghans, this chest also makes a fine coffee table when closed.

The blanket chest is a very simple project, made from four plywood panels, top and bottom panels and some decorative trim molding. For a nice, contemporary appearance, we chose to paint our blanket chest in soft pastel tones. If you paint your blanket chest as well, be sure to use glossy enamel paint—enamel paint finishes are easiest to clean. Another finishing option for the blanket chest is to line the interior with aromatic cedar liners to discourage moths and give blankets and other textiles a fresh scent. Aromatic cedar liners are sold in 4 × 8 sheets and self-adhesive strips.

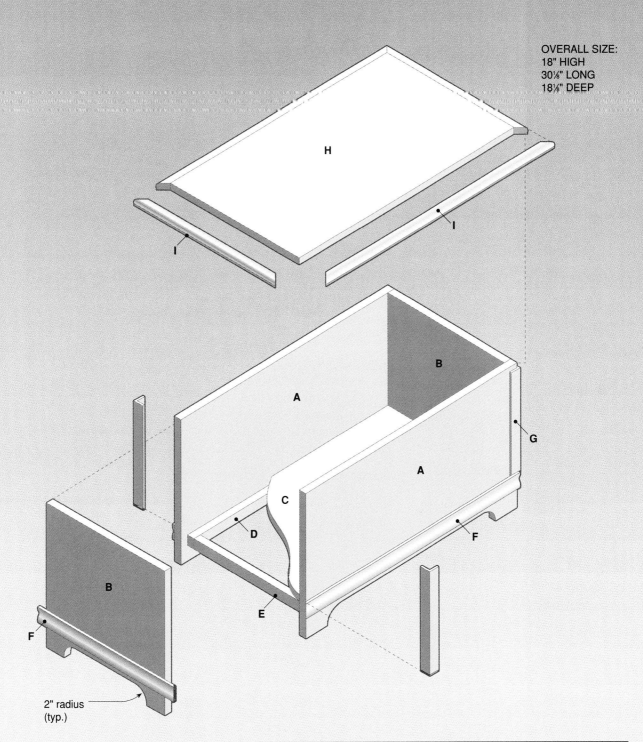

OVERALL SIZE:
18" HIGH
30⅛" LONG
18⅛" DEEP

2" radius
(typ.)

Key	Part	Dimension	Pcs.	Material
A	Side panel	¾ × 17¼ × 30"	2	Plywood
B	End panel	¾ × 17¼ × 16½"	2	Plywood
C	Bottom panel	¾ × 16½ × 28½"	1	Plywood
D	Side cleat	¾ × 1½ × 28½"	2	Plywood
E	End cleat	¾ × 1½ × 15"	2	Plywood

Cutting List

Key	Part	Dimension	Pcs.	Material
F	Bottom molding	½ × 1⅜ × *"	4	Stop molding
G	Corner molding	¼ × 1⁵⁄₁₆ × 12"	4	Corner molding
H	Lid	¾ × 18⅛ × 30⅛"	1	Plywood
I	Top cap	¾ × 1⅜ × *"	4	Shelf cap

Cutting List

Materials: Wood screws (#6 × 1¼", #6 × 2"), finish nails (4d), brads (¾", 1¼"), wood glue, finishing materials.

Note: Measurements reflect the actual thickness of dimensional lumber.

*Cut to fit.

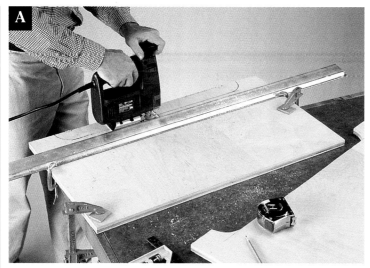

Use a jig saw and straightedge guide to make the scooped "kick space" cuts in the end and side panels.

worksurface, and make the cutouts with a jig saw **(photo A),** using a straightedge to guide the long straight portion of the cut. To draw the cutting lines for the kick spaces on the end panels, first draw cutting lines 2" up from one short edge. Use a compass to draw the curved cutting lines at the ends of each kick space; set the compass to draw a 2"-radius semicircle, and position the point of the compass as close to the bottom edge as possible, 4¼" in from the ends of the end panels. Draw the curved semi-circles, and make the cutouts with a jig saw. Sand the edges to smooth out any rough spots.

Directions: Blanket Chest

MAKE THE SIDES & ENDS. The side and end panels feature cutouts made on the bottom edges to create feet. Begin by cutting the side panels (A) and end panels (B) to size. To make the cutouts, or "kick spaces," on the bottom edges of the sides, first draw cutting lines on the sides, 2" in from one long edge. Use a compass to draw the curved cutting lines at the ends of each kick space; set the compass to draw a 2"-radius semicircle, and position the point of the compass as close to the bottom edge as possible, 5" in from the ends of the side panels. Draw the semi-circles. Clamp the sides to your

ASSEMBLE THE CHEST. Cleats are attached to the inside faces of the side and end panels, which are fastened together to form a basic chest. The cleats support the bottom panel of the chest, so it is important to attach them to the sides and ends with their top edges

Center the end cleats over the kick spaces, leaving ¾" at each end where the side cleats will fit.

Draw opposite chest corners together with a bar or pipe clamp to keep the chest square.

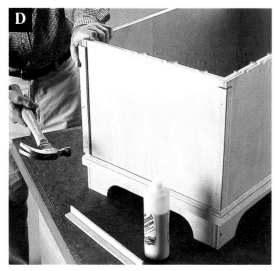

Fasten the corner molding over the corners to conceal the joints and screw heads.

Attach the top cap around the perimeter of the lid. Drive nails in partially before positioning the strips.

aligned. Cut the side cleats (D) and end cleats (E) to size. To help you position the cleats, draw reference lines on the side and end panels, 3½" up from the bottom edges and ¾" in from the side edges. Position the cleats so their top edges are flush with the reference lines, and fasten them with glue and #6 × 1¼" wood screws **(photo B),** driven through the cleats and into the panels. Countersink pilot holes in the cleats. With the cleats facing in, fasten the end panels between the side panels with glue and evenly spaced, countersunk #6 × 2" wood screws, forming a rectangular carcase. Make sure the top and bottom edges are flush, and the outside faces of the ends are flush with the side edges. Cut the bottom panel (C) to shape, and sand it smooth. Position the bottom onto the side cleats and end cleats, and clamp the panels together with a bar or pipe clamp. Check to to make sure the corners of the chest are square. Unclamp the panels, apply glue to the joints and clamp them back together.

Drive countersunk #6 × 2" wood screws through the sides and ends and into the bottom edges **(photo C).** To make sure you drive the screws directly into the bottom, mark the screw centerpoints 3⅞" up from the bottoms of the sides and ends before driving the screws.

ATTACH THE MOLDING. In order to cover the screws in the sides, ends and bottom, two different types of molding pieces are attached to the chest on the corners and along the bottoms of the side and end panels. Start by cutting the bottom molding (F) from ½ × 1⅜" stop molding. Cut the strips to fit around the sides and ends, 4⅜" up from their bottom edges, miter-cutting the ends of the pieces at 45° angles so they will fit together at the corners. Position the bottom molding on the sides and ends, and use glue and 4d finish nails to fasten it. Be sure you apply glue and drive nails through the joints where the molding pieces meet to "lock-nail" the pieces. Cut the corner molding (G) into ¼ × 1⁵⁄₁₆ × 12" pieces. Use glue and ¾" brads to fasten

the corner molding over the joints between the end and side panels **(photo D).** Make sure the bottom edges of the corner molding butt against the top edges of the bottom molding. Use a nail set to recess all the nails used to fasten the molding to the chest. We sanded the bottom edges of the corner molding to meet the bottom molding. Sand the top edges of the ends and sides to smooth the edges and corners.

MAKE THE LID. Cut the lid (H) to size, and sand it smooth. Cut four pieces of top cap (I) from ¾ × 1⅜" shelf cap molding to fit around the perimeter of the lid. Use glue and 4d finish nails to attach the top cap pieces, keeping the top edges flush **(photo E).** Glue and lock-nail the mitered corner joints. Set the lid into the top opening—no hinges are used.

APPLY FINISHING TOUCHES. Use a nail set to set all the nails and brads on the chest. Fill all visible nail holes with wood putty. Finish-sand the project to smooth out any rough spots. Finish as desired. We used a gloss enamel paint.

Art Deco Floor Lamp

Twin copper posts create dynamic contrast in this contemporary design.

Add a dash of style to a dark corner of your room with the Art Deco floor lamp. It's a striking addition that's as practical as it is beautiful. The overall design borrows from the long, fluid lines and curves of the Art Deco period, but is deceptively simple in construction. This project combines painted wood, copper tubing and easy-to-find electrical parts to create a singular, modern appeal. The thick half-lap joinery of the base makes an attractive and stable footing for the floor lamp, so accidental tipping won't be a constant worry. The most unusual aspect of the floor lamp is the copper used for the twin columns, made from ordinary water-supply pipe. Surprisingly inexpensive, the copper columns raise the lamp high enough so you can easily illuminate an entire room and, when polished, give off a brilliant shine. The columns also conceal the floor lamp's internal wiring, which leads up the base and columns and out through the top, where you install a lamp hardware kit (available at hardware stores). Various styles of globes or lamp shades can be combined with the floor lamp to complement almost any decor. We used a torchiere-style crystal lamp shade for a broad, warm glow and a contemporary look.

CONSTRUCTION MATERIALS

Quantity	Lumber
1	¾ × 3½" × 6' pine
1	¾ × 5½" × 6' pine
1	1½ × 5½" × 6' pine
2	1½"-outer-dia. × 6' copper tubing

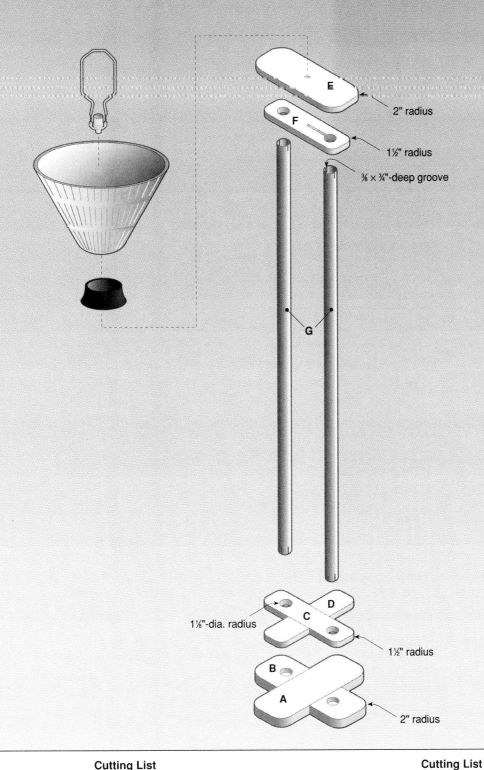

OVERALL SIZE:
60½" HIGH
15" WIDE
15" LONG

2" radius

1½" radius

⅜ × ¾"-deep groove

G

1⅛"-dia. radius

C

D

1½" radius

B

A

2" radius

Cutting List

Key	Part	Dimension	Pcs.	Material
A	Base bottom	1½ × 5½ × 15"	1	Pine
B	Base side	1½ × 5½ × 4¾"	2	Pine
C	Cross piece	¾ × 3½ × 13"	1	Pine
D	Cross trim	¾ × 3½ × 4¾"	2	Pine

Cutting List

Key	Part	Dimension	Pcs.	Material
E	Lamp seat	¾ × 5½ × 14¼"	1	Pine
F	Seat support	¾ × 3½ × 12¼"	1	Pine
G	Lamp column	1⅛"-dia. × 59½"	2	Copper tube

Materials: Finish nails (3d, 6d), wood glue, #6 × 1¼" wood screws, lamp hardware kit, lamp cord (10' min.), switch, plug, ⅜"-high plastic or rubber feet, wood putty, finishing materials.
Note: Measurements reflect the actual thickness of dimensional lumber.

Directions: Art Deco Floor Lamp

MAKE THE BASE PARTS. The lamp base is made of six rounded boards stacked in a half-lap pattern. Begin by cutting the base bottom (A), base sides (B), cross piece (C) and cross trim (D) to size. On the base bottom, mark lines 2" down and in from each corner, and draw 2"-radius curves at each intersection point. Do the same for two corners on a long edge of each base side. On the cross piece, mark lines 1½"

Drive nails near the ends of the cross piece to secure it to the base bottom and sides.

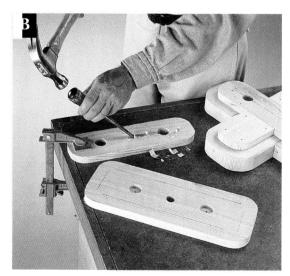

Chisel a groove for the lamp cord into the lamp seat.

down and in from each corner and on two corners on a short edge of the cross trim parts. Draw 1½"-radius curves at these points. Cut the curves with a jig saw, and sand the parts smooth.

ASSEMBLE THE BASE. Draw centerlines on the base bottom and base sides, across their short lengths. Align the base sides on either side of the base bottom so the curves face outward and the centerlines line up. Apply glue to the parts, and toenail them together with 4d finish nails. To help center the cross piece and cross trim, mark several 1"-deep location lines around the outer edges of the base pieces with a combination square or ruler. Center the cross piece over the base parts within the lines, and attach with glue and 6d finish nails **(photo A)**. Arrange the cross trim on either side of the cross piece, curves outward and centered within the 1" marks, and attach with glue and finish nails.

MAKE THE LAMP TOP. The top parts are rounded to match the base parts. Cut the lamp seat (E) and seat support (F) to size.

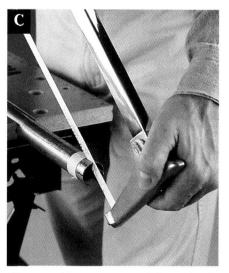

Wrap masking tape around the ends of the lamp columns to mark cutting depth.

Draw 2"-radius curves on the lamp seat corners, and 1½"-radius curves on the seat support corners, using the same method used for shaping the base pieces. Cut the curves with a jig saw, and sand smooth. Drill a ⅛"-dia. hole through the centerpoint of the lamp seat, and mark 1"-long location lines on the lamp seat face around the edges with a combination square. Clamp the seat support onto the lamp seat, centered within the location lines. Flip the clamped parts over, and drive a temporary 1¼" screw through the predrilled center hole, to hold the assembly together for the next step.

CUT COLUMN HOLES. Holes are drilled in the base and top parts for the lamp columns. If you are using alternative material for the lamp columns, such as metal conduit, be sure to measure the actual outside diameter to ensure a proper fit with the respective holes. Adjust the hole diameter, if necessary. Mark centerlines along the length of the cross piece and the seat support. Find the midpoint of each line, and make two marks 4⅛" from either side of the midpoint along the line. Use a 1⅛" spade bit to drill holes centered on these marks, 2" deep on the cross piece and 1½" deep on the seat support.

MAKE CORD PATHS. Holes and grooves on the base and top pieces allow the lamp cord to thread internally through the floor lamp (see *Diagram*, page 53 for additional reference). Disassemble the top parts and drill a

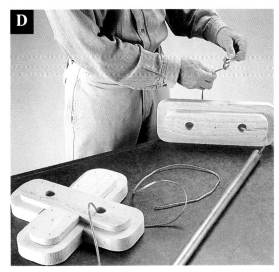

Tie a knot at each end of the lamp cord so it does not become unthreaded.

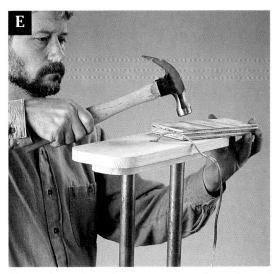

Use a piece of wood scrap to protect the surface of the lamp seat when securing it to the columns.

¾"-dia. hole through the lamp seat where the ⅛" hole is, to allow the lamp cord to pass to the lamp itself. On the seat support, chisel a ⅜"-dia. × ⅜"-deep groove, from the hole the screw left to one of the 1⅛" holes **(photo B).** The lamp cord will travel from the column to the lamp in this groove. With the groove facing the lamp seat, center the seat support back on the lamp seat and join the parts with glue and 4d finish nails. On the base parts, center and drill a ¾" hole completely through one of the 1⅛" holes so the lamp cord can exit the floor lamp.

MAKE THE LAMP COLUMNS. The copper lamp columns, made of rigid water-supply tubing, house the lamp cord. Slots are cut into the ends of the columns to aid assembly. Cut the lamp columns (G), using a tubing cutter or a hacksaw with a new blade. Designate top and bottom ends of the lamp columns. On the bottom of each lamp column, cut four 1"-deep slots in an "X"-shape. These slots will help strengthen the epoxy glue bond that secures the copper

tubing. On the top of one of the lamp columns, cut a ⅜"-wide × ¾"-deep groove into one side, to allow the lamp cord to flow into the groove of the seat support. Cut ¾"-deep slots in an "X"-shape in the tops of the lamp columns, including the end with the groove **(photo C).** Push one end of the lamp cord through the ¾"-dia. hole at the top of the lamp seat, and pull it out through the 1⅛"-dia. hole in the seat support. Feed the lamp cord through the lamp column with the ¾" groove, and run the cord out through the ¾"-dia. hole in the base assembly **(photo D).**

ATTACH THE LAMP COLUMNS. Rotate the corded column in the base until the groove in the top aligns with the grooved channel in the seat support. Make sure the groove is in the proper position before you attach the lamp columns to the base. Once you've determined the proper position, coat the holes in the base assembly with long-set epoxy (recommended for joining incongruous materials like metal and wood). Let the long-set epoxy set for at

least one hour, and then drive the lamp columns into the holes. Use a wood mallet or a piece of softwood to keep from bending the lamp columns. Be sure that the columns stay straight and perpendicular. When the glue has set, coat the holes in the seat support with epoxy, let set, and then drive the top assembly onto the lamp columns **(photo E).**

APPLY FINISHING TOUCHES. Let the epoxy dry completely. Fill all holes and gaps with wood putty, and sand all surfaces smooth. Apply primer and paint to the base and top, and allow to dry. Attach a switch and plug to the lamp cord near the base, and install your lamp hardware kit according to the manufacturer's instructions. Use copper polish on the columns, or rub them with an abrasive pad and then seal with car wax or paste wax. Or you can choose to leave the copper unfinished, and in time it will develop a light, greenish patina. Finally, attach ⅜"-high plastic or rubber feet to the base to allow the lamp cord to freely exit the floor lamp.

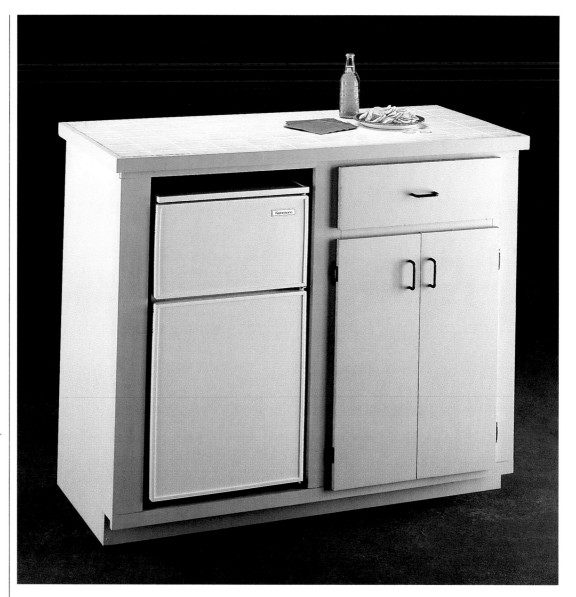

Snack Center

*Custom cabinetry with a convenient countertop, this snack center
will add a new dimension to your family room.*

CONSTRUCTION MATERIALS

Quantity	Lumber
2	¾" × 4 × 8' plywood
5	1 × 2" × 8' pine
3	1 × 4" × 8' pine
1	¼" × 2 × 4' lauan plywood
1	¼" × 2 × 5' tile board
1	¾ × ¾" × 4' stop molding

This snack center, essentially a small pantry, establishes a special place for snacks within the family room. The snack center stores treats within easy reach, while eliminating back-and-forth trips to the kitchen (and the risk of spills on the way). This project is open-backed, and should be positioned against a wall. A refrigerator fits snugly on the left side of the cabinet to keep drinks, dips and other chilled snacks fresh and tasty. Behind the cupboard doors lies plenty of room for plates, napkins and dry foods like mixed nuts or chips. A sliding drawer keeps utensils organized, and the tileboard top provides an easy-cleaning prep area, perfect for slicing fruits, cheeses or cakes.

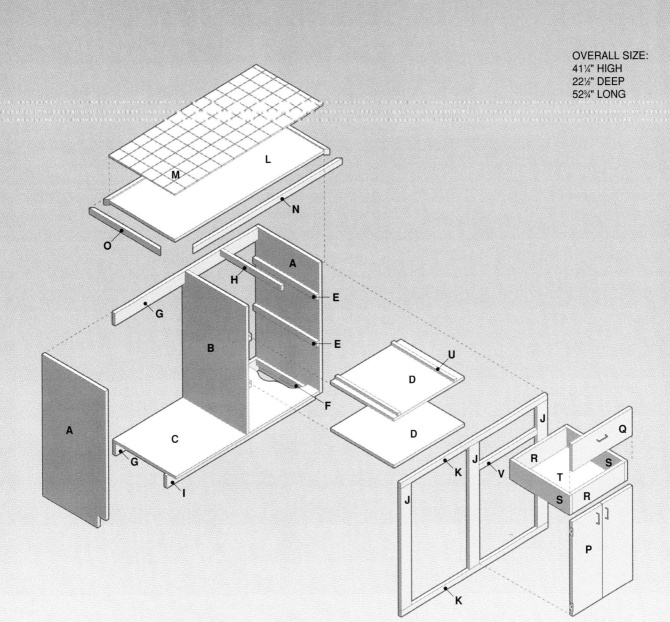

Cutting List

Key	Part	Dimension	Pcs.	Material
A	Side panel	¾ × 21¾ × 41¼"	2	Plywood
B	Center divider	¾ × 21¾ × 37"	1	Plywood
C	Bottom panel	¾ × 21¾ × 49½"	1	Plywood
D	Shelf	¾ × 21¾ × 24⅜"	2	Plywood
E	Long cleat	¾ × 1½ × 21¾"	4	Pine
F	Short cleat	¾ × 1½ × 18"	2	Pine
G	Back rail	¾ × 3½ × 49½"	2	Pine
H	Retainer	¾ × 1½ × 21"	1	Pine
I	Kick rail	¾ × 3½ × 51"	1	Pine
J	Stile	¾ × 3½ × 35½"	3	Pine
K	Rail	¾ × 1½ × 51"	2	Pine

Cutting List

Key	Part	Dimension	Pcs.	Material
L	Countertop	¾ × 22¾ × 51¼"	1	Plywood
M	Surface	¼ × 22¾ × 51¼"	1	Tileboard
N	Long trim	¾ × 1½ × 52¾"	2	Pine
O	Short trim	¾ × 1½ × 24¼"	2	Pine
P	Door	¾ × 10⅝ × 27¾"	2	Plywood
Q	Drawer front	¾ × 7 × 21⅜"	1	Plywood
R	Drawer end	¾ × 6½ × 18½"	2	Plywood
S	Drawer side	¾ × 6½ × 21½"	2	Plywood
T	Drawer bottom	¼ × 20 × 21½"	1	Lauan plywood
U	Drawer guide	¾ × ¾ × 21¾"	2	Stop molding
V	Small rail	¾ × 1½ × 20¼ "	1	Pine

Materials: Wood glue, #6 wood screws (1¼", 1⅝"), finish nails (4d, 6d), 1" brads, ⅜" set-back overlay hinges (4), door and 3" wire door pulls (3), panel adhesive, finishing materials.

Note: Measurements reflect the actual thickness of dimensional lumber.

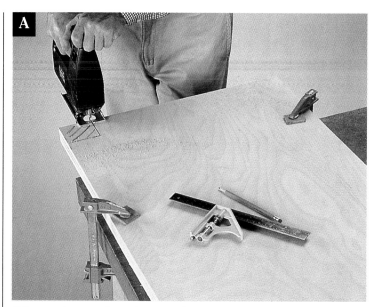

is attached to the lower front of the snack center in a later step. Cut out notches at these outlines with a jig saw **(photo A).** From one corner on the center divider, mark a line 3½" down along one long edge, and ¾" in along the short edge to make another notch outline. Cut out this notch with a jig saw. Next, draw reference lines for shelf cleats across the inside of each side panel, 3½" up from the bottom edge. Mark reference lines for the shelf cleats on the right face of the center divider and the inside face of the right side panel, 9" and 22½" down from the top edges. Drill countersunk pilot holes 2" in from each end of each cleat, and also in the middle of each cleat. Using glue and 1¼" screws, attach the short cleats to the lower part of each side panel, ¾" in from the back edge, so the top is flush with the reference line. Attach the long cleats so the tops are flush with the remaining reference lines that are marked on the center divider and the right

When cutting notches, clamp each piece to your worksurface to ensure smooth, even cuts.

Directions: Snack Center

MAKE THE SIDE PANELS & CENTER DIVIDER. The side panels and the center divider are fitted with shelf cleats that also assist in the assembly of the cabinet. The panels also must be notched to accept back rails which will connect the pieces and tie the cabinet together. Begin by cutting the side panels (A), center divider (B), long cleats (E) and short cleats (F) to size, and sand all parts to smooth out any rough edges. On one corner of each side panel, mark a line 3½" down along one long edge, and mark another line 3" in along the short edge, forming rectangular cutout outlines—the outlines create the notches that are cut out to hold the kick rail, which

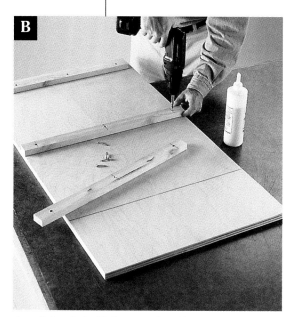

Attach 1 × 2 shelf cleats to the side panels and cabinet divider.

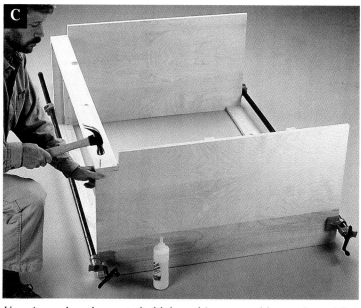

Use pipe or bar clamps to hold the cabinet assembly together while you attach the kick rail in the front notches.

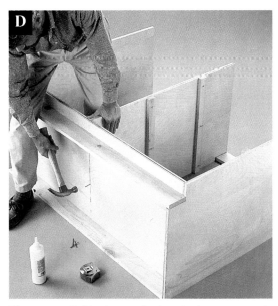

The center divider is attached to the bottom panel with glue and finish nails.

The lower rail of the face frame overhangs the bottom panel slightly.

side, using glue and 1¼" wood screws **(photo B).**

ATTACH THE SIDE & BOTTOM PANELS. The sides are connected by a front kick rail and two back rails. The bottom panel is then attached, keeping the assembly square. Cut the kick rail (I), back rails (G) and bottom panel (C) to size, and sand the parts smooth. Use a pair of pipe clamps or bar clamps to hold the back rails between the two sides, and attach the kick rail to the notched-out area on the fronts of the sides using glue and 6d finish nails **(photo C).** Then, fasten each back rail in place with glue and finish nails, making sure the top back rail edges are flush with the upper side corners. The top edge of the lower back rail should be flush with the short cleats. The bottom panel rests on top of the short cleats and the lower back rail, inside the cabinet frame. Unclamp the assembly and stand it on edge. Apply glue to the tops of the short cleats and

around the lower back support and kick rail, and position the bottom panel in place. Attach it with 1¼" screws driven through the bottom panel and into the short cleats.

ATTACH THE CENTER & SHELVES. Reference lines drawn on the bottom panel help to attach the center divider, and shelves are then installed on the snack center. Cut the shelves (D) to size, and sand

TIP

The snack cabinet design accommodates a refrigerator with maximum dimensions of 20¼ x 21¾ x 35½". Measure to make sure your refrigerator will fit within this space. Refrigerators, like all household appliances, generate some heat, so you should leave spaces of at least ½" around all sides of the refrigerator for ventilation. This protects both the appliance and the snack center.

smooth. On the top face of the bottom panel, measure over 24⅜" from the right-hand side and mark a line across the short side of the bottom panel. Draw a similar line at 24⅜" on the upper back rail. On the bottom of the bottom panel, measure over 24" from the right-hand cleat, and draw another line across the short side of the bottom panel. Position the center divider inside the cabinet so the notch fits over the back rail, and the edge of the center panel is flush with the reference lines. Fasten the center panel first to the back rail with glue and 6d finish nails. Lay the cabinet on its back, and make sure the center divider is straight. Attach the center divider to the bottom panel with glue and finish nails driven along the bottom reference line and into the edge of the center divider **(photo D).** Install the shelves on the long cleats with glue and 6d finish nails, so the shelf edges are flush with the cleats.

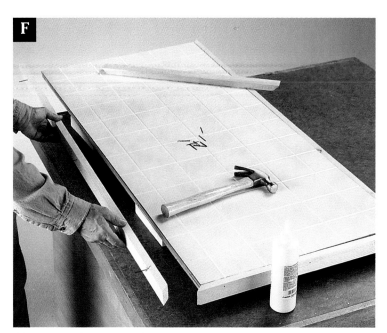

Use pieces of scrap wood as spacers to raise the countertop off your worksurface. This makes attaching the trim pieces easier.

Use pipe or bar clamps to secure the drawer parts together.

ATTACH THE TRIM PIECES. Trim pieces fastened to the front provide a more finished look. The frame created by the trim pieces is called the *face frame* by those who are familiar with cabinetmaking (see *TIP*, page 61). Cut the rails (K), small rail (V), retainer (H) and stiles (J) to size, and sand smooth. Attach one rail to the front of the cabinet across the top edge of the side panels and center divider, using glue and 6d finish nails. Make sure that the cabinet is square when attaching the rail. Position two of the stiles along each side panel edge so the edges are flush and the tops butt against the upper rail. Fasten the stiles to the side panel edges with glue and finishing nails. Center the middle stile on the edge of the center divider, and glue and nail in place, making sure that the space between the edges of the center and right stiles is 20¼". After attaching the stiles, glue

and nail the lower rail in place **(photo E).** The bottom edge of the lower rail should overlay the lower corners of the sides. Butt the face of the small rail against the edge of the upper shelf so the tops are flush, and fasten using glue and finish nails. Place the retainer between the upper rail and the back support to keep the drawer from tilting when it is pulled out. Adjust the bottom edge of the retainer so it's even with the bottom edge of the top rail, and fasten with glue and finish nails.

MAKE THE COUNTERTOP. The plywood countertop is covered with a sheet of tileboard, providing an easy-to-clean, spill-resistant surface. Cut the countertop (L), surface (M), long trim (N) and short trim (O) to size, and sand the wood parts to smooth any rough edges—cutting the tileboard with a straightedge and utility knife should yield a nice

clean edge. Instead of cutting the trim pieces to the exact sizes shown in the *Cutting List* on page 57, we suggest that you cut the trim pieces slightly long and then cut the pieces to exact length as you miter-cut the ends to fit around the countertop. Temporarily place the tileboard on the countertop. Attach the trim so it is flush with the top of the tileboard surface, using glue and 4d finish nails driven into the edges of the plywood countertop **(photo F).**

MAKE THE DRAWER. The drawer fits into an opening in the top, right side of the cabinet. If you intend to store flatware and utensils in the drawer, purchase a drawer organizer. Cut the drawer front (Q), drawer ends (R), drawer sides (S) and drawer bottom (T) to size, sanding smooth any jagged edges. On a flat worksurface, clamp the drawer ends between the drawer sides with a pipe clamp, and join the parts with glue and 6d finish nails **(photo G).** Fasten the drawer bottom to the drawer frame with glue and 1" brads.

MAKE & ATTACH THE DOORS. Two hinged doors cover the lower shelf and protect the contents of the cabinet from dust. Cut the doors (P) to size. Attach hinges to the doors, 2" in from each edge, so the barrels are flush with the edges. Adjust the doors on the stiles so they are centered over the cabinet opening, with an equal amount of overlap over the small rail and the bottom rail. Attach the doors, and install a 3" wire door pull on each door, 3" down from the top of the doors, and 1¼" in from where the doors meet.

INSTALL THE DRAWER. Drawer guides are installed on the top shelf next to the drawer sides, to provide a groove or channel for the drawer to slide in and out of, and to prevent sideways motion. Cut the drawer guides (U) to size. Center the drawer in the drawer opening, and place a drawer guide on each side of the drawer. Arrange the pieces close to the drawer, but leave enough space so the drawer will slide easily. (There should be about a 1½"-gap between each drawer guide and the shelf edge.) Drill countersunk pilot holes and attach the drawer guides to the shelf with glue and #6 × 1¼" screws. Drill countersunk pilot holes through the outer end of the drawer so the drawer front can be attached from the inside. Clamp the drawer front to the drawer and adjust so the front is in line with the doors and is centered over the drawer opening **(photo H).** Attach the

TIP

If you have experience building cabinets, you may find it unusual to construct the face frame (comprised of the stiles and rails) of the snack center piece by piece as we described. An option for more advanced woodworkers is to build the cabinet first without the stiles and rails, assemble these parts into a face frame, and then attach it as a whole to the front of the cabinet.

drawer front to the drawer with # 6 × 1¼" screws driven through the predrilled pilot holes in the drawer end and into the drawer front. Attach a door pull in the center of the drawer front—the pull should be the same size and style as the pulls you will attach to the cabinet doors.

APPLY FINISHING TOUCHES. Remove the tileboard surface from the top assembly. Attach the plywood countertop to the cabinet with glue and # 6 × 1⅝" screws. Remove or mask all of the hardware. Fill any screw holes, nail holes or voids in the edges of plywood with wood putty. Sand all surfaces smooth with medium-grit sandpaper, then give them a quick sanding with fine-grit paper. Apply a coat of wood primer, then paint the snack center. We used latex enamel with a high gloss (glossy paint is easier to clean than flat or semi-gloss paint). When the paint has dried, apply panel adhesive or tileboard adhesive to the plywood countertop (both products are usually sold in cartridges and applied with a caulk gun). Set the tileboard into the adhesive, then roll with a wallpaper roller or J-roller, working from the center out, to create a smooth, bubble-free surface.

Make sure the drawer is square and centered in the opening, then position the drawer front.

Liquor Locker

PROJECT
POWER TOOLS

Store spirits of all varieties safely behind lock and key in this beautiful oak cabinet.

Compact and elegant, this liquor locker provides protected storage for liquor or cordials, without looking like a bank safe. Made from oak and oak plywood, this functional furnishing has a formal style that features arched cabinet doors. A simple cylinder lock installed in one of the door frames keeps your alcohol products away from curious young hands.

The main compartment in the liquor locker is sized to hold several full-size bottles of your favorite liquors, cordials and aperitifs. A narrow shelf in the back of the compartment is perfect for storing mixers that usually come in smaller bottles, like bitters, vermouth or lime juice. Or, you can stow glassware on the shelf. The top sur-face of the cabinet is made from oak plywood. It is large enough to provide an ample surface for preparing or serving after-dinner drinks in your den. To accentuate the natural tones of the red oak, we did not stain the wood, and we applied a clear topcoat of water-based polyurethane. When choosing your topcoating product, note that some types, like shellac and paste wax, are dissolved by alcohol.

CONSTRUCTION MATERIALS

Quantity	Lumber
1	¾" × 4 × 8' oak plywood
1	½" × 2 × 4' oak plywood
1	1 × 2" × 8' oak
1	1 × 4" × 6' oak
2	2 × 2" × 8' oak
1	¾ × ¾" × 6' cove molding
2	⅜ × ¾" × 8' base shoe molding

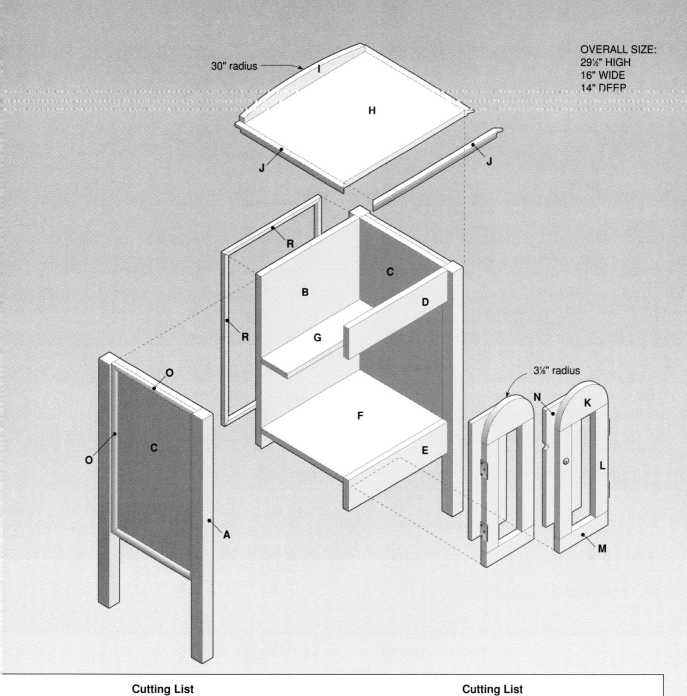

OVERALL SIZE:
29½" HIGH
16" WIDE
14" DEEP

30" radius

3⅛" radius

	Cutting List			
Key	**Part**	**Dimension**	**Pcs.**	**Material**
A	Leg	1½ × 1½ × 27¼"	4	Oak
B	Back panel	¾ × 13 × 19¼"	1	Plywood
C	Side panel	¾ × 11 × 19¼"	2	Plywood
D	Top rail	¾ × 3½ × 13"	1	Oak
E	Bottom rail	¾ × 2 × 13"	1	Oak
F	Bottom panel	¾ × 11 × 13"	1	Plywood
G	Shelf	¾ × 3½ × 13"	1	Oak
H	Top panel	¾ × 14 × 16"	1	Plywood

	Cutting List			
Key	**Part**	**Dimension**	**Pcs.**	**Material**
I	Backsplash	¾ × 1½ × 16"	1	Oak
J	Top molding	¾ × ¾ × *"	3	Cove molding
K	Top door rail	¾ × 3½ × 6¼"	2	Oak
L	Door stile	¾ × 1½ × 12"	4	Oak
M	Lower door rail	¾ × 1½ × 6¼"	2	Oak
N	Door panel	½ × 4¼ × 13"	2	Plywood
O	Side trim	⅜ × ¾ × *"	10	Base shoe molding

Materials: Wood screws (#6 × 2", #6 × 2½"), 1¼" brass brads, 1" wire nails, 8d finish nails, wood glue, 1½ × 3" brass hinges (4), cylinder lock hardware, 2" brass corner brackets (6), elbow catches (2), finishing materials.

Note: Measurements reflect the actual thickness of dimensional lumber.
*Cut to fit.

Directions: Liquor Locker

MAKE THE CABINET SECTION. The legs are the main structural members for the cabinet. We used oak plugs to conceal the screw holes, so we counterbored all visible pilot holes. Start by cutting the legs (A), back panel (B) and side panels (C) to size. Arrange the legs in pairs, and position a side panel between the legs in each pair. One short edge of each side

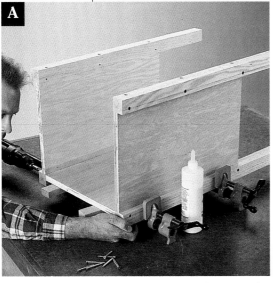

panel should be flush with the tops of the legs. Drill pilot holes, and attach the sides between the legs with glue and #6 × 2½" brass wood screws, driven through the legs and into the edges of the side panels. Set the back panel on your worksurface, supported by ¾"-thick scraps. Butt the leg pairs against the edges of the back panel, making sure the tops are flush. Apply glue, and clamp the leg pairs to the back panel with bar or pipe clamps. Attach the legs to the back with #6 × 2½" brass wood screws **(photo A).** Cut the top rail (D), bottom rail (E) and bottom panel (F) to size. Fasten the top rail between the legs with glue and #6 × 2½" wood screws, with the top and inside edges flush. Attach the bottom rail to the front edge of the bottom panel with the tops flush. Apply glue to the edges of the bottom panel and bottom rail, and insert them into the cabinet: the top edge of the bottom rail should be 10¼" up from the bottoms of the legs. Drill pilot holes, and fasten the bottom

Set the back panel on spacers, clamp it between the rear legs and fasten it with glue and wood screws.

panel and bottom rail with #6 × 2" wood screws. Like the sides, back and top rail, the front face of the bottom rail should be ¾" back from the outsides of the legs. Measure diagonally from corner to corner to make sure the cabinet is square **(photo B).** If the measurements are the same, the frame is square. Cut the shelf (G) to size, and position it so the bottom face is 7" up from the bottom panel. Attach the shelf with glue and wood screws, driven through the back and side panels.

MAKE THE TOP. The top is made from plywood and edged with oak cove molding. Begin by cutting the top panel (H) and backsplash (I) to size. The peak of the curved backsplash, located at the midpoint, should be 1½" up from the bottom edge. To draw a smooth, even curve onto the backsplash, drive a finish nail partway into the board at the peak of the curve, then drive nails at the starting points of the curve, ½" up from the bottom edge of the backsplash. Slip a flexible

Measure from corner to corner to check for square. If the project isn't square, apply pressure to one side or the other until it is square.

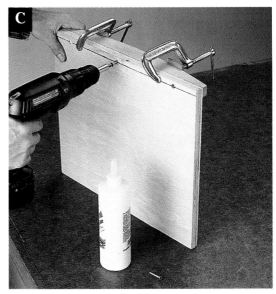

Apply glue, clamp the backsplash in place, and attach it to the top.

straightedge behind the nails at the starting points and in front of the nail at the peak to create a smooth curve. Trace along the inside of the straightedge to make a cutting line. Cut the curve with a jig saw, and sand it smooth. Clamp the back-splash to the top panel so the side and back edges are flush. Drill pilot holes, apply glue, and fasten the backsplash to the top with #6 × 1¼" brass wood screws **(photo C).** Cut the top molding (J) to size, miter-cutting the front ends of the side pieces and both ends of the front piece. Apply glue to the top molding, and attach it with brads, forming miter joints at the front corners. Drill pilot holes to avoid splitting the molding. Center the top panel over the cabinet, with the back edges flush. Clamp the top in place, and secure it with six 2" brass corner brackets, spaced evenly on the inside faces of the side and back panels.

MAKE THE DOORS. The cabinet doors are frame-and-panel style. The frames feature an arched rail at the top, and the door panels are attached to the backs of the frames. Start by cutting the top door rails (K) to length. Use a compass to draw a 3¼"-radius semicircle on each rail, centered ¼" up from the bottom edge of the rail. The tops of the semicircles should just touch the top edges of the boards. Cut along the semi-circles with a jig saw, and gang-sand both arches smooth with a belt sander to remove any saw marks. Cut the door stiles (L) and lower door rails (M) to size. After sanding them smooth, drill pilot holes, and attach the door rails to the bottoms of the door stiles with

glue and #6 × 2" wood screws, driven through the bottom edges of the door rails and into the door stiles. To complete the door frames, position the semi-completed frame on your worksurface, and butt the arched rails against the free ends of the door stiles. Apply glue, and clamp the frame together with bar clamps. Check the frame to make sure it is square. Drill pilot holes, and attach the arched top rails to the door stiles with 8d finish nails, driven through the tops of the rails and into the door stiles **(photo D).** When the glue has dried on the frame, drill a hole for a cylinder lock through the front face of one door stile, using a backing board to prevent splintering when the bit exits the door stile on the other side. The lock hardware we used required a ⅞"-dia. hole, 3½" below the top of the arched rail. Cut the door panels (N) to size. Draw reference lines on one face of each door frame, ½" in from the inside edges. Position the panels within these lines. To accommodate the lock hole on one frame, cut a notch in the panel with a jig saw. Sand the panels, then attach them to the frames with glue and 1" wire nails.

APPLY FINISHING TOUCHES. Cut the side trim (O) pieces to length from ¾" base shoe molding. Miter-cut the ends at 45° angles to make miter joints at the corners. Use glue and 1¼" brads to attach the trim so it butts against the sides and legs, and along the bottom edge of each side. Also frame the back panel with base shoe molding. Set and fill all nail holes. Fill all screw holes with wood plugs, and finish-sand the project. In-

stall two brass 1½ × 3" hinges on each door, 1" up from the door bottom and 1" down from the top rail. Fasten the hinges to the legs, making sure the doors overlap the bottom rail by ¾". Install the lock. Fasten elbow catches at the top and bottom to secure the door that does not contain the lock **(photo E).** Cover the hardware with masking tape, and apply your finish of choice. We used clear polyurethane.

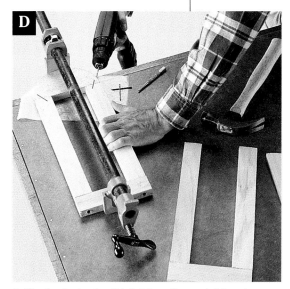

Drill pilot holes for 8d finish nails, and drive them through the joint between the arch and stiles.

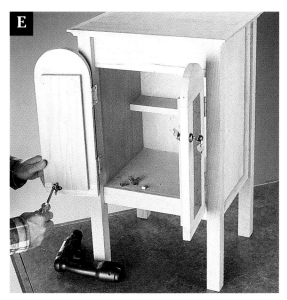

Attach elbow catches to the door that does not contain the lock.

PROJECT
POWER TOOLS

Secretary Topper

*Transform a plain table, desk or cabinet top into a fully
equipped secretary with this box-style topper.*

In the furniture world, a secretary is a self-standing, upright cabinet with a drop-down worksurface that conceals numerous storage cubbies when raised. The traditional secretary also has two or three large drawers at the bottom. With this secretary topper, we zeroed in on the cubbyhole feature, creating a simple storage unit that will convert just about any flat surface into a functioning secretary.

The fixed shelves are designed to accommodate papers all the way up to legal size. The adjustable shelf can be positioned for address and reference books. The vertical slats with the cutout dividers are for storing incoming or outgoing mail. And the handy drawer is an ideal spot to keep stamps, sealing wax and other small desktop items.

We made this simple wood project from oak and oak plywood. If you are building a secretary topper to fit on top of an existing piece of furniture, try to match the wood type and finish as best you can.

NOTE: This secretary topper is sized to fit snugly atop the Writing Desk featured on pages 12 to 17.

CONSTRUCTION MATERIALS

Quantity	Lumber
1	¼" × 2' × 3' oak plywood
2	1 × 10" × 8' oak
1	½ × 8" × 6' oak
1	¼ × 2" × 7' oak mull casing

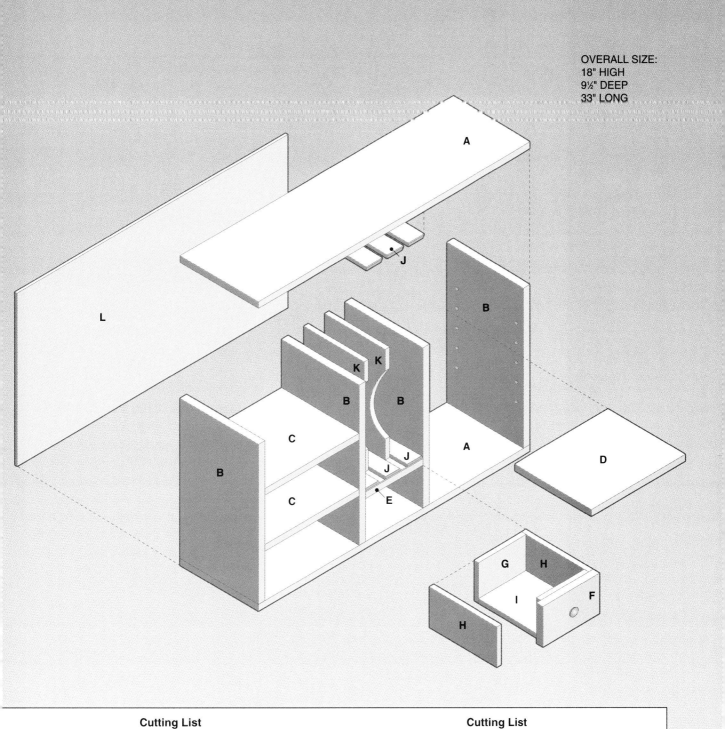

OVERALL SIZE:
18" HIGH
9½" DEEP
33" LONG

A			
L			
B			
C			
K	K		
B	B		
J	J		
E		A	D
C			
G	H		
I	F		
H			

Cutting List

Key	Part	Dimension	Pcs.	Material
A	Top/bottom	¾ × 9¼ × 33"	2	Oak
B	Partition	¾ × 9¼ × 16½"	4	Oak
C	Fixed shelf	¾ × 9¼ × 11½"	2	Oak
D	Adjustable shelf	¾ × 9¼ × 11¼"	1	Oak
E	Bin top	¾ × 9¼ × 7"	1	Oak
F	Drawer front	¾ × 4⅛ × 6¾"	1	Oak

Cutting List

Key	Part	Dimension	Pcs.	Material
G	Drawer end	½ × 4⅛ × 5¾"	2	Oak
H	Drawer side	½ × 4⅛ × 8¼"	2	Oak
I	Drawer bottom	½ × 5¾ × 7¼"	1	Oak
J	Bin spacer	¼ × 2 × 9"	6	Mull casing
K	Divider	½ × 7¼ × 11½"	2	Oak
L	Back panel	¼ × 17⅞ × 32¾"	1	Plywood

Materials: #6 × 2" wood screws, brads (¾", 1"), wood glue, ¼"-dia. shelf pins (4), ¾"-dia. brass knob (1), adhesive felt pads (6), finishing materials.

Note: Measurements reflect the actual thickness of dimensional lumber.

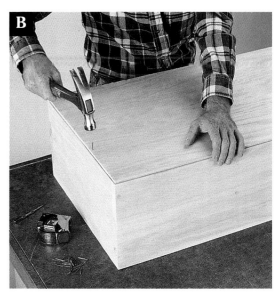

Use pegboard as a drilling template to make sure shelf pin holes in the partitions align.

Fasten the back panel to the secretary cabinet with wire brads, squaring as you go.

Directions:
Secretary Topper

MAKE THE SHELF FRAME-WORK. The shelf framework is made by attaching two shelves and a bin top between three vertical partitions. Start by cutting the partitions (B), fixed shelves (C) and bin top (E) to size. Sand the parts after cutting to remove any saw marks or rough spots. Draw reference lines across the faces of two partitions, 5" in from one short edge and 5¾" in from the other short edge. Drill counterbored pilot holes, and use glue and #6 × 1⅝" wood screws to fasten the shelves between the two partitions with their bottom edges flush with the reference lines. Draw reference lines on the outside face of one of the attached partitions, 4¼" up from the bottom edge. Use glue and wood screws to fasten the bin top to the partition, with its bottom edge on the reference line. Make sure the front and rear edges are flush, then fasten an unattached partition to the free end of the bin top with glue and wood screws, keeping the edges flush. The final section contains an adjustable shelf. To drill holes in the partitions to hold the shelf pins, clamp a piece of pegboard to one face, and use it as a drilling template (photo A) to drill ¼"-dia. × ⅜"-deep holes into the partitions. After you drill holes in one partition, mark the locations of the pegboard holes you used with tape, and repeat with the opposing partition. Keep the same end up and the same edge in front. Wrap masking tape around your drill bit as a bit stop to keep you from drilling through the partitions. Sand the assembly smooth.

COMPLETE THE CABINET. The top and bottom panels, a back panel and an outer partition are added to wrap the shelf framework, forming a cabinet. Cut the top/bottom panels (A) to size. Attach a panel to the ends of the partitions at the top and at the bottom of the frame-work. Fasten the remaining partition between the top and bottom panels, making sure the outside face is flush with the ends of the shelf framework. Cut the back (L) to size. Sand the edges, and then fasten the back to the cabinet with ¾" brads (photo B). Fasten one end of the back first, then check for square. Adjust if needed, then finish attaching the back panel.

MAKE THE DRAWER. The drawer parts are made from ½"-thick oak stock and are cut to size by rip-cutting a ½ × 8"-wide board. Start by cutting the drawer front (F), drawer ends (G), drawer sides (H) and drawer bottom (I) to size. Sand the edges, and fasten the drawer ends between the drawer sides with glue and ¾" brass brads, driven through the drawer sides and into the drawer ends. Make sure the outside faces of the drawer ends are flush with the ends of the drawer sides. Position the drawer bottom inside the drawer ends and drawer sides. Drill pilot holes, and fasten the drawer bottom with ¾" brads (photo C). Do not use glue to attach the bottom. Cut the

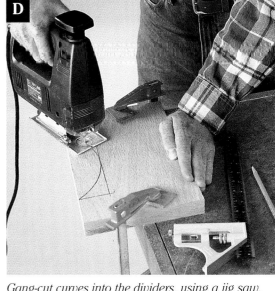

The drawer is made from ½"-thick wood, so be sure to drill pilot holes for the nails.

Gang-cut curves into the dividers, using a jig saw.

drawer front (F) to size, and center it on one drawer end. With the edges flush, attach the drawer front with glue and brass brads, driven through the end and into the front. Sand all the edges, and test-fit the drawer into the bin.

INSTALL VERTICAL DIVIDERS. Cut the bin spacers (J) and dividers (K) to size. The bin dividers are made from ¼"-thick × 2"-wide oak mull casing, which is frequently used with patio doors. Draw a curve on the front edge of one divider: start the curve 2¼" in from the top and bottom edges, and make the curve 2" deep at the center. Clamp the dividers together with their edges flush, and gang-cut them along the curved cutting line with a jig saw **(photo D).** Sand the dividers while they are still clamped, using a drum sander attachment on an electric drill. The bin spacers have bevels sanded into their front edges. A belt sander mounted on its side grinds bevels quickly. Clamp a scrap guide to your worksurface to stabilize the parts as

you grind them, making sure the sanding belt is perpendicular to the surface. Use the scrap as a guide to steady the workpieces as you grind bevels on the front edges of the spacers **(photo E).** Use ¾" brads to fasten two of the bin spacers to the bin top, flush against the partitions. Fasten two more bin spacers to the top. Insert the dividers, and fasten the last bin spacers between them. Remove the dividers for finishing.

APPLY FINISHING TOUCHES. Cut the adjustable shelf (D) to size. Fill all counterbored holes with glued oak plugs. Finish-sand all wood surfaces. Apply a finish of your choice. We used linseed oil. When the finish is dry, attach a ¾"-dia. brass knob to the drawer front. Insert the shelf pins and adjustable shelf. Attach adhesive-backed felt buttons to the bottom of the secretary topper to prevent scratching your desk.

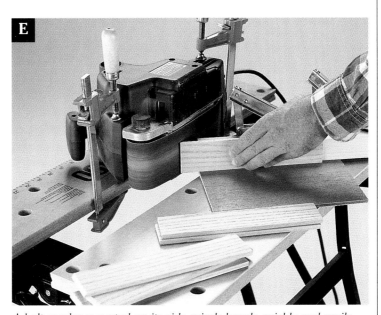

A belt sander mounted on its side grinds bevels quickly and easily.

Deacon's Bench

*At home in the family room, library or entry, this traditional bench
provides convenient seating and hidden storage.*

CONSTRUCTION MATERIALS

Quantity	Lumber
1	¾" × 4 × 8' birch plywood
1	1 × 4" × 8' pine
2	1 × 6" × 8' pine

With a bench seat that flips up to expose a storage compartment, this deacon's bench is a great place for storing phone books, favorite novels or a lap-top computer—best of all, it provides some roomy seating in the process. Perfect for an unused nook of your den or family room, or even in the hallway, the deacon's bench makes the most of a traditional design, combining functional seating with convenient storage. And you can throw a few pillows onto the bench seat to add another level of comfort and style as you take advantage of a quiet moment to relax, call a friend or get a little extra work done at home.

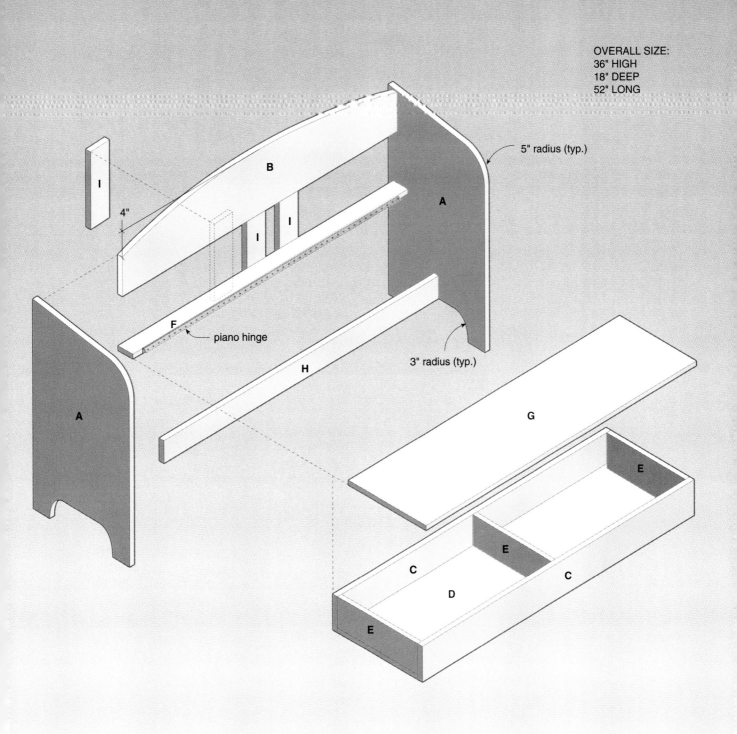

OVERALL SIZE:
36" HIGH
18" DEEP
52" LONG

5" radius (typ.)

4"

piano hinge

3" radius (typ.)

Cutting List				
Key	Part	Dimension	Pcs.	Material
A	End panel	¾ × 18 × 32½"	2	Plywood
B	Backrest	¾ × 10 × 50½"	1	Plywood
C	Seat rail	¾ × 5½ × 50½"	2	Pine
D	Bottom	¾ × 14½ × 50½"	1	Plywood
E	Lid support	¾ × 4¾ × 14½"	3	Pine

Cutting List				
Key	Part	Dimension	Pcs.	Material
F	Hinge rail	¼ × 2¾ × 50½"	1	Plywood
G	Lid	¾ × 14¼ × 50¼"	1	Plywood
H	Bottom rail	¾ × 3½ × 50½"	1	Pine
I	Slat	¾ × 3½ × 12"	3	Pine

Materials: Wood screws (#6 × 1¼", #6 × 2"), wood glue, ¾" birch edge tape (50'), 1½ × 48" piano hinge, finishing materials.

Note: Measurements reflect the actual thickness of dimensional lumber.

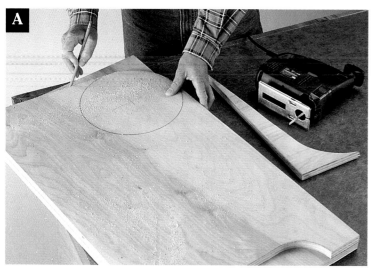

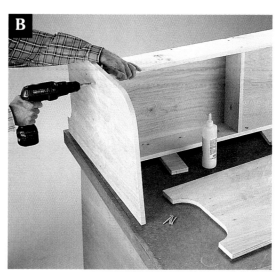

After cutting one end panel to shape, use it as a template for marking cutting lines onto the other end panel.

Fasten the seat frame between the end panels with glue and wood screws.

Directions: Deacon's Bench

MAKE THE END PANELS. Cut all plywood parts from birch plywood, using fine-tooth blades on your circular saw and jig saw, then apply self-adhesive veneer edge tape to the exposed edges to give them a smooth, finished appearance. Countersink all the screws; you will fill the screw holes with wood putty before you paint the project. Start by cutting the end panels (A) to size. Designate a top, bottom, front and back to each end. The best way to ensure uniform end panel shapes is to make the cuts on one end panel, then trace its shape onto the other end panel. To cut the arches on the bottom edges of the end panels, start by setting a compass to draw a 3"-radius semicircle. Set the point of the compass as close to the bottom edge as possible, 6" in from the front edge, and draw the semicircle. Draw another 3"-radius semicircle on the bottom edge, 6" in from the back edge. Draw a straight cutting line connect-

ing the tops of the two semi-circles, and cut along the cutting line with a jig saw. The tops of the end panels slant downward from front to back and have a rounded top, front corner. Use a compass to draw a 5"-radius circle near the top, front corner; position the point of the compass 7" down from the top edge and 5" in from the

front edge. Draw the circle, then draw a straight line from the top, rear corner to the top of the circle. Cut along the line with a jig saw, and sand the cuts smooth. Position the finished end panel on top of the uncut end panel, and trace the shape **(photo A).** Cut the second end panel to shape with a jig saw, and sand it smooth.

Attach the slats to the backrest and hinge rail, maintaining a 1½"-wide gap between slats.

MAKE THE BACKREST. The backrest fits between the end panels and has a sweeping arc cut along the top edge. Cut the backrest (B) to size, and use a thin, flexible straightedge to draw an arc at the top. Drive one finish nail at the center of the top edge and another along each side edge, 4" down from the top edge. Hook the straight-edge around the center nail and inside the nails along the sides. Trace the arc with a pencil, then cut it with a jig saw. Sand the edges smooth. Use a household iron to apply self-adhesive veneer edge tape to the front and back edges of the ends, and to the top and bottom edges of the backrest.

MAKE THE SEAT. The seat is a simple rectangular frame with a plywood bottom. The frame is made by attaching three lid supports between two seat rails, flush with their top edges. Cut the lid supports (E) and seat rails (C) to size. Position two lid supports between the seat rails so their outside faces are flush with the ends of the seat rails. Drill pilot holes, and fasten the seat rails with glue and #6 × 1¼" wood screws, driven through the seat rails and into the lid supports. Center the remaining lid support between the seat rails, and fasten it with glue and wood screws. Cut the seat bottom (D) to size, and fasten it in place in the recess formed between the bottom edges of the lid supports and the bottom edges of the seat rails. Next, mark reference lines on the ends, 11¾" and 17¼" up from the bottom edges. Stand the seat frame on a seat rail, supported by a ¾"-thick scrap

board. Apply glue to the outside face of the outside lid supports. Set the ends on their back edges, and position them against the outside lid supports so the frame is centered between the reference lines. Drive #6 × 2" wood screws through the ends and into the lid supports to secure the parts **(photo B)**. Set the backrest on a ¾"-thick piece of scrap, and fasten it between the ends so the bottom edge of the backrest is 26" up from the bottoms of the ends. Use glue and wood screws, driven through the ends and into the backrest to attach the backrest between the ends.

ATTACH THE RAILS & SLATS. The rails are attached between the ends. One rail is positioned near the bottoms of the end panels to add strength to the project. Another rail is positioned on the back seat rail—this rail will be attached to a long hinge when you attach the seat lid. Finally, decorative vertical slats are fastened to the bench to span the gap between the backrest and seat. Start by cutting the bottom rail (H) to size. Position the bottom rail between the ends so it is centered and its bottom edge is flush with the top of the arch. Cut the hinge rail (F) to size, and sand it smooth. Stand the

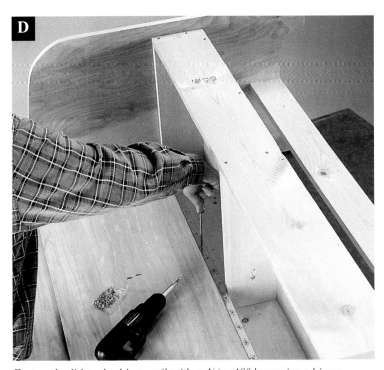

Fasten the lid to the hinge rail with a 1½ × 48"-long piano hinge.

bench upright, and fasten the hinge rail between the end panels; the bottom of the hinge rail should sit squarely on the seat frame, and the back edge of the hinge rail should be ¾" in from the back edges of the end panels. Cut the slats (I) to size, and sand them smooth. Center the first slat between the end panels, and attach it with glue and #6 × 1¼" wood screws. Fasten a slat on each side of the middle slat so there are 1½"-wide gaps between slats **(photo C)**.

APPLY FINISHING TOUCHES. Cut the lid (G) to size. Apply veneer edge tape to all the edges, and sand the lid smooth. Use a 1½ × 48"-long piano hinge to fasten the lid to the hinge rail **(photo D)**. Remove the hinge, and fill all countersunk holes with wood putty. Finish-sand the project, and finish as desired. We applied a semi-gloss latex paint. Reinstall the piano hinge.

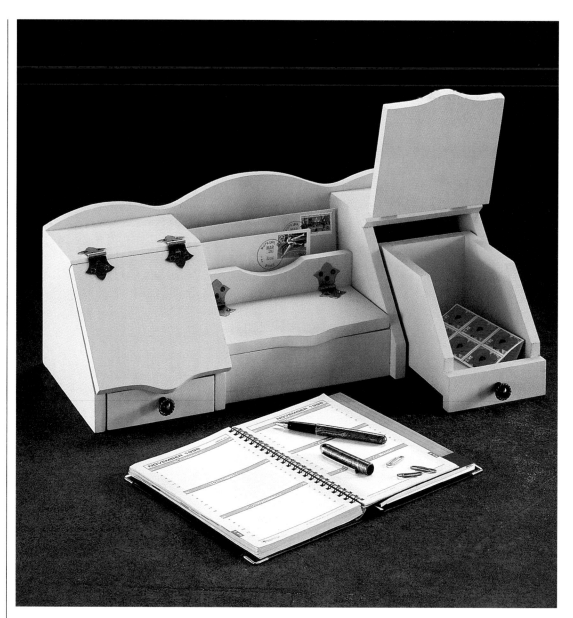

Desktop Console

*Decorative accents and efficient design
replace your desktop clutter.*

Quantity	Lumber
1	1 × 8" × 8' pine
1	1 × 4" × 3' pine
1	½ × 1¾" × 3' cove molding

Designed to keep your desktop necessities organized and ready to use, this desktop console features four separate storage compartments. The middle section contains a covered pencil holder made from cove molding, while the two side compartments are pull-out drawers for notepads, stationery or ad-

dress books. A fourth compartment behind the pencil holder acts as a mail slot. The drawers are completely removable so you can have access to their contents without having to reach all the way into the narrow compartments. Paint the project to match your den, and use decorative hinges and knobs on the lids and drawers.

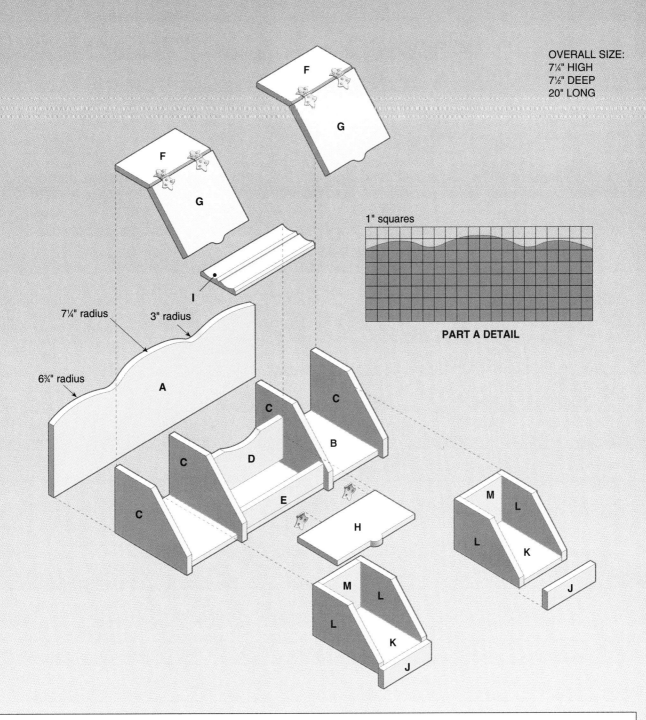

OVERALL SIZE:
7¼" HIGH
7½" DEEP
20" LONG

1" squares

PART A DETAIL

7¼" radius

3" radius

6¾" radius

Cutting List

Key	Part	Dimension	Pcs.	Material
A	Back	½ × 7¼ × 20"	1	Pine
B	Bottom	½ × 6½ × 19"	1	Pine
C	Divider	½ × 5½ × 7"	4	Pine
D	Letter holder	½ × 3½ × 8"	1	Pine
E	Front	½ × 1½ × 8"	1	Pine
F	Top	½ × 4 × 6"	2	Pine
G	Lid	½ × 6 × 6"	2	Pine

Cutting List

Key	Part	Dimension	Pcs.	Material
H	Pencil cover	½ × 4½ × 7¾"	1	Pine
I	Pencil holder	⁹⁄₁₆ × 1¾ × 8"	2	Cove molding
J	Drawer front	½ × 1½ × 4¾"	2	Pine
K	Drawer bottom	½ × 3¾ × 6"	2	Pine
L	Drawer side	½ × 4¼ × 6½"	4	Pine
M	Drawer back	½ × 3¾ × 4¼"	2	Pine

Materials: 1" brads, wood glue, ¾"-dia. brass knobs (2), 1⁵⁄₁₆ × 2¼" ornamental hinges (6), finishing materials.

Note: Measurements reflect the actual thickness of dimensional lumber.

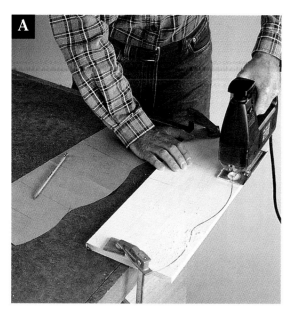

Trace the grid pattern onto the back, and cut the back to shape with a jig saw.

Shade in the waste areas on the dividers so you don't make cutting mistakes when cutting the slanted profiles.

Directions:
Desktop Console

MAKE THE BACK. The back and letter holder are first cut to size, then shaped with a jig saw on their top edges. A pattern is used to trace the shape onto the back, while a compass is all that is needed to draw the letter holder profile. Start by cutting the back (A) to size. Draw a 1"-square grid pattern onto a sheet of sturdy paper, then copy the profile for the back, using the pattern on page 75 as a guide. Center the template over the back, and trace around the cutout shape. Cut the back to shape with a jig saw **(photo A).** Sand the edges of the back to smooth out any saw marks or rough edges. Cut the letter holder (D) to size. Use a compass to draw a 3"-radius curve on the board, making sure the lowest point of the curve is ½" down from one long edge. The curve should intersect the edge of the board 2¼" in from each end. Cut the

Position the front between the interior dividers, and fasten it with glue and brads.

curve with a jig saw. Sand the curve to smooth out any rough edges.

MAKE THE DIVIDERS. Four dividers separate the console into sections and form the niches for the drawers. The two interior dividers are notched on their bottom edges so they

can fit onto the bottom. Cut the dividers (C) to size. Designate one long edge of each divider as the top, and one short edge as the back. Use a pencil to mark the top edge, 3½" in from the back. Make another mark on the front edge, 1½" up from the bottom. Draw a straight line

TIP

An extremely helpful tool when making intricate cuts is the scrolling jig saw. The blade on a scrolling jig saw can be manipulated independently from the position of the saw body—you can change the direction of the cut without changing the direction of the saw. A scrolling saw increases your control when cutting and is ideal for difficult jig saw work.

connecting the marks, and shade in the triangular section formed by the line. Later, you will trim this section off to form the finished slanted profiles of the dividers. Next, make the cutting lines for the two dividers that are notched on their bottom edges to accommodate the bottom (B). To make the cutting lines for the notches, first draw a line across two dividers, ½" up from the bottom edge. Start these cutting lines at the backs of the dividers, and end them ½" in from the front edges. Shade the area between the bottom edge and the cutting line **(photo B),** and use a jig saw to cut out the shaded areas on the dividers. Sand all the edges to smooth out any rough spots.

ASSEMBLE THE FRAME. The frame is made by attaching the back to the bottom, and then fastening the dividers. Cut the bottom (B) and front (E) to size. Center the back against a long edge of the bottom. Drill pilot holes, apply glue and drive evenly spaced 1" wire brads through the back and into the bottom. The back should extend ½" past the bottom at each end of the board. Fasten the letter holder (with the curved edge up) between the notched dividers, flush with

the bottom edges of the dividers. The rear face of the letter holder should be 2" in from the back edges of the dividers. Position the notched dividers and letter holder on the bottom: make sure the dividers are butting flush against bottom and back. The outside faces of the notched dividers should be 5" in from the ends of the bottom. Fasten the notched dividers with glue and 1" brads, driven through the bottom and back, and into the

dividers. Position the front between the dividers, flush with the front edge of the bottom. Attach it with glue and brads **(photo C).** Apply glue to the ends of the bottom and the rear edges of the outside dividers, and butt them against each end of the bottom. Drive 1" wire brads through the ends and into the bottom.

MAKE THE TOPS, LIDS & PENCIL COVER. The tops (F), lids (G) and pencil cover (H) form the hinged assemblies on the top of the project. The lids and pencil cover have slight decorative curves on their front edges. The tops are beveled on their front edges, allowing the lids to swing open for drawer use. Begin by cutting the tops, lids and pencil cover to size. Designate a front and back on the lids and pencil cover, and draw a reference line across

Clamp a belt sander to your worksurface, and use it as a grinder to cut bevels into the front edges of the tops.

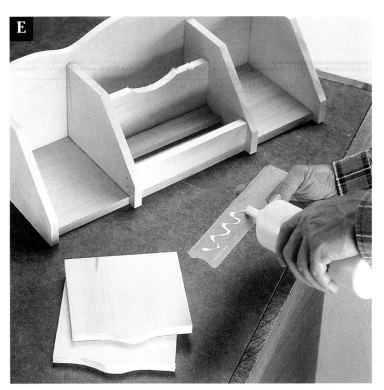

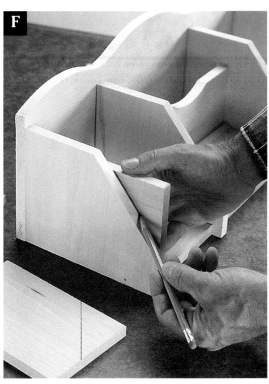

Apply glue to the bottoms of the pencil holders, and press them into place between the dividers.

Position the drawer sides against the inside faces of the ends, and trace the profiles.

them, ½" in from the front edges. Use a compass to draw a centered arc on each reference line: the tops of the arcs should face the front edges of the lids and pencil cover to create a small scallop, or handle, on the workpieces (see *Diagram*, page 75). Cut along the reference lines and arcs with a jig saw, and sand the edges smooth. On the tops, draw a reference line ½" in from the front edge. Clamp a belt sander with a medium-grit sanding belt to your worksurface, and make a bevel on the front edges, sanding from the top face down to the reference line **(photo D).** Cut the pencil holders (I) to size from ⁹⁄₁₆ × 1¾" cove molding. Apply glue to the bottom faces of the molding, and fasten the pencil holders between the front and letter holder **(photo E).**

TIP

You have a number of options to keep drawers working smoothly. Tack-on drawer glides, for instance, are available at most woodworker's stores. You can also periodically rub beeswax on the drawer bottoms; or, you can attach Teflon® tape to the drawer bottoms.

MAKE THE DRAWERS. Two small drawers are built to fit between the dividers. The drawers must be made to conform with the slanted profiles of the dividers. On the completed project, the lids will flip up, allowing access to the drawers. Cut the drawer fronts (J), drawer bottoms (K), drawer sides (L) and drawer backs (M) to size. Position a drawer side on top of the bottom (B). Make sure the front

edge of the drawer side is flush with the front edge of the divider, and trace the slanted profile of the divider onto the drawer side **(photo F).** Cut the drawer side to shape, and sand it smooth. Using the finished drawer side as a tracing template, draw cutting lines onto the remaining drawer sides. Cut them to shape with a jig saw. Position the drawer backs between the drawer sides with their bottom edges flush, and fasten the pieces **(photo G).** Next, test-fit the drawer bottoms to make sure the front edges are flush with the drawer sides. Fasten the drawer bottoms between the drawer sides with glue and brads. Finally, attach the drawer fronts to the front edges of the drawer sides and bottoms. Make sure the

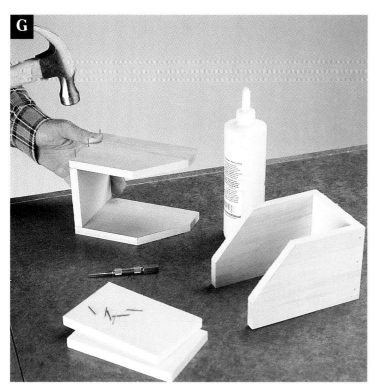

Fasten the drawer backs between the drawer sides with glue and wire brads.

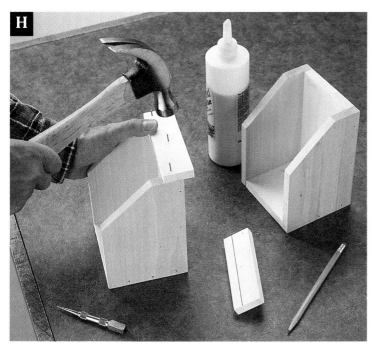

Attach the drawer fronts to the front edges of the drawer sides and drawer bottoms so they overhang the bottoms by ½".

of the drawer fronts so they are flush with the bottom edges of the bottom board.

APPLY FINISHING TOUCHES. Use glue and brads to attach the tops (F) to the top edges of the dividers with the bevels on the front edges, facing the bottom of the project. Make sure the tops butt directly against the back and are flush with the outside faces of the ends. Use a file or belt sander to create a slight bevel on the top, front edges of the lids: when combined with the larger bevels on the bottom faces, the small bevels allow the lids to swing open fully. Tape the lids in place against the tops, test-fitting the pieces to make sure the bevels mate. If needed, sand the joints until they fit together. Fill all the holes in the project with wood putty. Sand all the surfaces with medium (100- or 120-grit) sandpaper to smooth out any rough spots, then finish-sand with fine (150- or 180-grit) sandpaper. Prime and paint the desktop console—cover all the surfaces with an enamel paint. Fasten the lids to the tops, using $1\frac{5}{16} \times 2\frac{1}{4}$" brass ornamental hinges. Fasten the pencil cover to the divider in the same way. Attach $\frac{3}{4}$"-dia. decorative brass (screw-in-type) knobs to the drawer fronts, and insert the drawers between the ends.

bottom edges of the drawer fronts extend ½" down from the bottom edges of the drawer sides, creating a lip that overhangs the front of each drawer **(photo H).** It will help to draw a reference line, ½" up from one long edge. Test-fit the drawers between the ends. If needed, sand the bottom edges

Humidor Cabinet

Keep cigars and pipe tobacco fresh inside this attractive humidor cabinet.

PROJECT
POWER TOOLS

Despite the considerable health risks associated with smoking, increasing numbers of people today are allowing themselves the simple luxury of a fine cigar after a meal or a bowl of pipe to-

CONSTRUCTION MATERIALS

Quantity	Lumber
1	¾" × 4 × 4' plywood
4	1 × 2" × 6' aspen
1	½ × 7" × 3' aspen panel

bacco enjoyed with a snifter of cognac or sherry. The social ritual of the after-dinner cigar shared in the den or study is a large part of the appeal to today's casual smokers. With that appeal in mind (as well as the desire to keep tobacco products fresh), we've designed this humidor cabinet.

The humidor is a very traditional den furnishing. Its distinguishing characteristics are a lined compartment that traps moist air, preventing tobacco

from becoming dry and stale, as well as a heat-resistant top for holding ashtrays.

This humidor cabinet differs from most humidors because the tobacco compartment is removable. Creating a sealable compartment with a hinged door is difficult unless you want to use complex woodworking joinery. So we chose to build a separate, simple compartment that can be sealed to keep moisture in, then inserted into the cabinet.

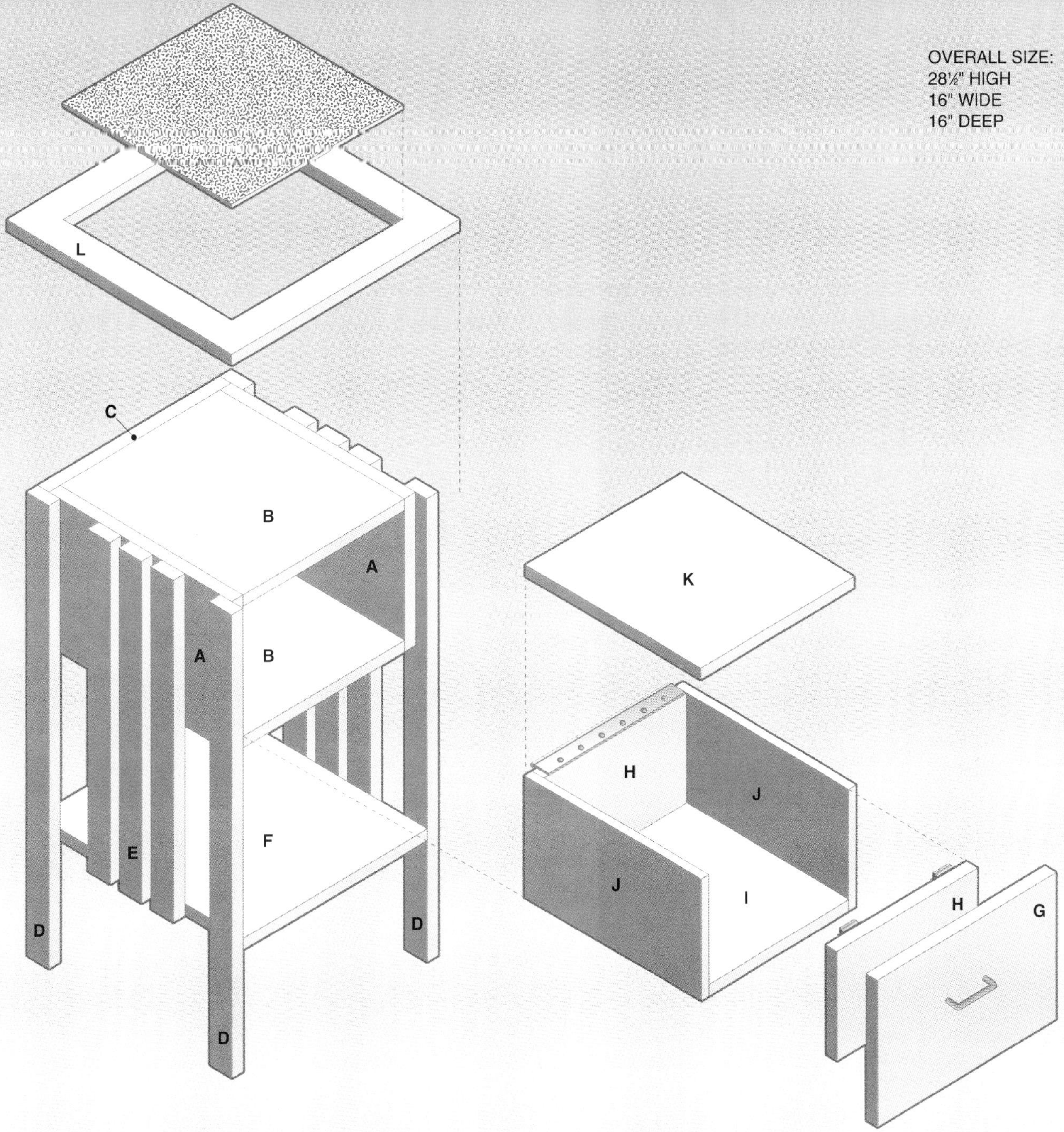
OVERALL SIZE:
28½" HIGH
16" WIDE
16" DEEP
L
C
B
A
A
B
E
F
D
D
D
K
H
J
J
I
H
G

Cutting List

Key	Part	Dimension	Pcs.	Material
A	Side panel	¾ × 9 × 13"	2	Plywood
B	Cabinet panel	¾ × 11½ × 13"	2	Plywood
C	Back panel	¾ × 9 × 13"	1	Plywood
D	Leg	¾ × 1½ × 27¾"	4	Pine
E	Slat	¾ × 1½ × 20½"	6	Pine
F	Shelf	¾ × 12⅞ × 14½"	1	Plywood

Cutting List

Key	Part	Dimension	Pcs.	Material
G	Box front	¾ × 8¾ × 12¾"	1	Plywood
H	Box end	¾ × 5⅝ × 10"	2	Plywood
I	Box bottom	¾ × 10 × 12½"	1	Plywood
J	Box side	½ × 6⅜ × 12½"	2	Pine
K	Box lid	¾ × 11 × 12⅜"	1	Plywood
L	Top frame	¾ × 16 × 16"	1	Plywood

Materials: Wood screws (#6 × 2", #6 × 1¼"), finish nails (3d), wood glue, chest handle, drawer pull, ¾" birch edge tape (10'), light-duty brass piano hinge, tack-on drawer glides, 12" ceramic floor tile, grout, mortar, magnetic catches (2), finishing materials.

Note: Measurements reflect the actual thickness of dimensional lumber.

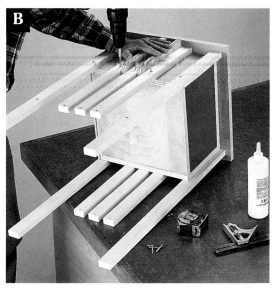

Fasten the back panel to the side and end panels with glue and wood screws.

As you attach the slats, use scrap spacers to maintain consistent gaps between the slats.

Directions:
Humidor Cabinet

MAKE THE CASE. The case is an open-sided cabinet that houses the humidor box. The top of the case also serves as the top of the project. The cabinet supports a large ceramic floor tile inside a square cutout. Cut the side panels (A), cabinet panels (B) back panel (C) and top frame (L) to size. Use a household iron to apply edge tape to one short edge of each side and cabinet panel, and all four edges of the top frame. Trim and sand the taped edges smooth. The top frame holds a piece of ceramic tile. Before marking the cutout on the top frame, measure the tile, then add ¼" to each dimension for the cutout. Use a combination square to draw cutting lines across the top frame, 2" in from each edge. Drill a starter hole inside the cutting lines, and make the cutout with a jig saw. Next, draw reference lines on the top frame, 1½" in from each edge to help you position a cabinet panel beneath it. Apply glue, and position a cabinet panel against the top frame inside the reference lines. Drive 3d finish nails through the cabinet panel and into the top frame. Use glue and wood screws to fasten the remaining cabinet panel between the side panels so the edges are flush. Position the top frame onto the sides, and drive wood screws through the side panels and into the edges of the cabinet panel. NOTE: Arrange the screws so the heads will be covered by the legs and slats later in the assembly process (see *Diagram*, page 81). Fasten the back panel to the side and end panels with glue and countersunk #6 × 2" wood screws **(photo A).**

BUILD THE STAND. The stand is made by attaching a leg at each corner of the cabinet, then adding decorative vertical slats. A shelf is fastened between the legs to help stabilize the project and add a small storage space. Cut the legs (D), slats (E) and shelf (F) to size. Apply veneer edge tape to all the shelf edges. Trim and sand the parts smooth after cutting. Designate a top and bottom end on each leg. Draw a reference line across each leg 7¼" up from the bottom end. Drill pilot holes, and use glue and countersunk #6 × 1¼" wood screws to attach the legs and slats to each side panel. Make sure the front legs overhang the front edges of the side panels by ¾" and the back legs are flush with the back edges of the cabinet. The legs and slats should butt up against the underside of the top. Center the slats between the legs, and use ¾"-thick scrap spacers to maintain even gaps between the slats as you attach them **(photo B).** Position the shelf between the legs, flush with the reference lines, and attach it with #6 × 2" wood screws, taking care to avoid previously inserted screws.

MAKE THE HUMIDOR BOX. The humidor box is an enclosed unit with a hinged top. The design is similar to the case, but a large front piece fits over one end. The top of the

A 10"-long piano hinge joins the box lid to the box end.

TIP

Maintain the humidity in your humidor by keeping a damp sponge or a dish of water inside. If you want to monitor the humidity level closely, gauges for humidors are available at specialty stores.

humidor box is hinged. To get access to the contents of the box, just pull the humidor box out of the case, and open the top. Cut the box front (G), box ends (H), box bottom (I), box sides (J) and box lid (K) to size. Apply edge tape to all the box front edges, box lid edges and one box bottom edge. Position a box end face to face against the box front. Make sure the box end is centered on the box front, and fasten it with glue and #6 × 1¼" wood screws driven through the box end and into the box front. Set the box bottom on your worksurface, and position a box side squarely against one long edge with the edges flush. Fasten the box side with glue and countersunk wood screws, driven through the box side and into the box bottom. Attach the remaining box side, using the same method. Set the remaining box end between the box sides. The outside face of the box end should be flush with the ends of the box sides and box bottom. Fasten the box end with glue and wood

screws. Position the box sides against the box front. The front box end should fit between the box sides and butt against the box bottom. Apply glue, and fasten the front in place with #6 × 1¼" wood screws, driven through the sides and into the box end. Center a 10"-long piano hinge at the end of the box lid. The barrel of the hinge should be aligned with one short edge of the box lid. Fasten the hinge to the box lid, and then attach the box lid to the rear box end **(photo C).**

APPLY FINISHING TOUCHES. Fill all nail holes and screw holes with wood putty. Sand the surfaces smooth, and apply your finish of choice—we used enamel paint. Mount magnetic catches on

the inside of the box end and corresponding plates on the box lid. Attach a drawer pull handle to the front of the humidor box and a chest handle to the rear end. Install drawer glides inside the cabinet to allow the humidor box to slide easily **(photo D).** If you want the tile top to be flush with the frame, attach a piece of ¼"-thick plywood to the top cabinet panel. Mix thin-set mortar, and apply a ⅜"-thick layer with a notched trowel. Set the tile into the mortar bed. Let the mortar dry overnight, then fill the gaps between the tile and top frame with tinted grout. Mask the frame before applying the grout. To effectively contain moisture inside the humidor, line the box with light-gauge copper or tileboard, fastened to the inside walls of the box with construction adhesive.

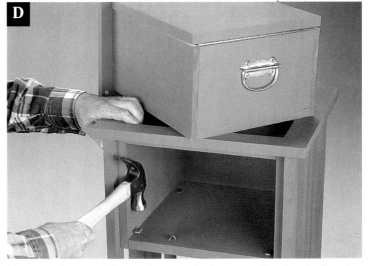

Tack the drawer glides in place inside the case, allowing the humidor box to slide in and out easily.

TV Buddy

*From remote controls to coasters, this handy organizer has a space
for just about any accessory used by serious television enthusiasts.*

CONSTRUCTION MATERIALS

Quantity	Lumber
1	¼" × 1 × 2' plywood
1	1 × 10" × 6' pine
1	1 × 2" × 6' pine
1	¾ × ¾" × 2' pine
2	¾ × ¾" × 7' pine cove molding

From those who take their television seriously, but don't want their TV essentials cluttering up the family room, this handy organizer will get top ratings. On a coffee table or end table, this TV Buddy has compartments and cubbies sized to hold just about everything that's important to the pastime of watching

TV: remote controls, guides and program listings; coasters and even beverage containers all can be stowed very neatly and efficiently.

Next time you're rummaging through your family room trying to find that perpetually missing remote control, you'll understand the appeal of this original project idea.

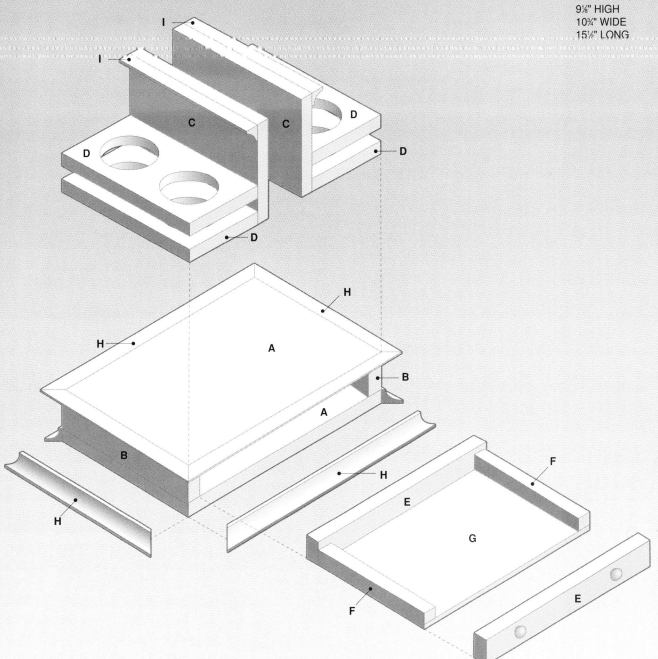

OVERALL SIZE:
9⅛" HIGH
10¾" WIDE
15½" LONG

Cutting List

Key	Part	Dimension	Pcs.	Material
A	Base panel	¾ × 9¼ × 14"	2	Pine
B	End board	¾ × 1⅝ × 9¼"	2	Pine
C	Rack side	¾ × 6 × 9¼"	2	Pine
D	Holder	¾ × 5 × 9¼"	4	Pine
E	Drawer face	¾ × 1½ × 12¼"	2	Pine

Cutting List

Key	Part	Dimension	Pcs.	Material
F	Drawer side	¾ × ¾ × 7¾"	2	Stop molding
G	Drawer bottom	¼ × 7¾ × 12⅛"	1	Pine
H	Base molding	¾ × ¾ × *"	8	Cove molding
I	Rack molding	¾ × ¾ × 9¼"	2	Cove molding

Materials: Wood screws (#6 × 1¼", #6 × 1⅝"), brads (¾", 1¼"), wood glue, ⅜"-dia. brass knobs (4), finishing materials.

Note: Measurements reflect the actual thickness of dimensional lumber.
*Cut to fit.

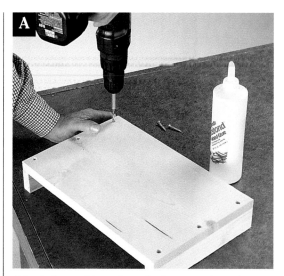

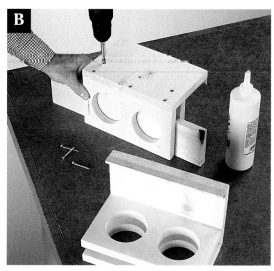

Attach the end boards to the bottom of one base with glue and screws, keeping the edges flush.

Slide a scrap wood spacer between the holders to maintain the space while fastening the rack.

Directions: TV Buddy

BUILD THE BASE SECTIONS. Three elements make up the base: the base, rack and holders. Begin by cutting the base panels (A) and end boards (B) to size. Sand the parts after cutting to smooth out any rough edges. NOTE: The ends are easily cut to size by rip-cutting a 1 × 4" pine board in half, using a circular saw and straightedge cutting guide. Position one base panel on the end boards so the edges are flush. With the outside faces of the ends flush with the short edges of the base panel, fasten the parts with glue and countersunk #6 × 1¼" wood screws **(photo A).** Cut the racks (C) and rack molding (I) to size. Position a piece of rack molding against each rack so the molding is flush with one long edge. Attach the rack molding to the racks with glue and ¾" brads. Use a nail set to recess the brads below the surface. Cut the holders (D) to size. Each holder contains two circular cutouts for holding beverage containers or remote controls. Using a compass,

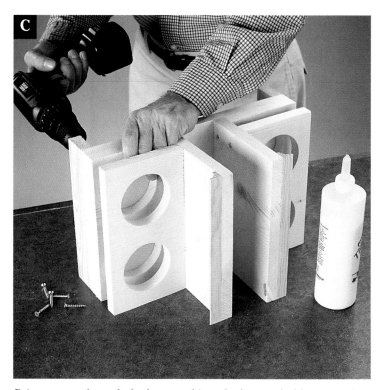

Drive screws through the base and into the bottom holders, securing the holders and rack.

draw two centered, 1½"-radius circles on each holder. When drawing the circles, place the point of the compass 2½" in from each edge. Drill ⅜"-dia. starter holes within the circles, and use a jig saw to make the circular cutouts. Sand the holders to smooth out any saw marks.

ATTACH THE RACKS & HOLDERS. Two holders are attached to each rack. To fasten the parts, position one holder against a rack so the edges are flush. One face of the holder should be flush with a long edge of the rack. The holder should be on the same face

Use glue and 1¼" brads to attach the drawer faces to the drawer sides and drawer bottom.

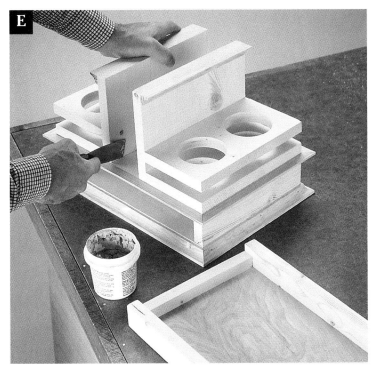

Fill all visible screw and nail holes with wood putty. Sand to create a smooth surface for painting.

edges to mark centers for wood screws. Position the racks on the base so their outside edges are flush with the base edges. Drill pilot holes, and use glue and countersunk wood screws, driven through the base and into the bottom holders, to attach the workpieces **(photo C).** Finally, attach the remaining base to the ends so the edges are flush. Sand all the surfaces smooth.

MAKE THE DRAWER. A shallow drawer fits in the gap between the bases. It is a simple rectangular frame with a plywood bottom. Begin by cutting the drawer faces (E), drawer sides (F) and drawer bottom (G) to size. Set the drawer sides on your worksurface, 12" apart. Fasten the drawer bottom to the sides with glue and ¾" brads, making sure the sides are flush with the short edges of the drawer bottom. Fasten the drawer faces to the drawer bottom and drawer sides, using glue and 1¼" brads **(photo D).** The bottom edges of the drawer faces should be flush with the drawer bottom.

APPLY FINISHING TOUCHES. Cut the base molding (H) to fit around the edges of both bases. Miter-cut the ends of the base molding pieces at 45° angles to fit together at the corners. Use glue and 1¼" brads to fasten the molding pieces to the bases, keeping the top edges flush. Fill all nail and screw holes with untinted wood putty **(photo E).** When the wood putty is dry, finish-sand all the surfaces smooth. Apply a gloss enamel paint. Attach brass, ⅜"-dia. knobs to both drawer faces.

as the rack molding. Fasten the holder with glue and #6 × 1¼" wood screws, driven though the rack and into the holder. Set a ¾"-thick scrap wood spacer against the attached holder, and butt an unattached holder squarely against it. Apply glue, and fasten the second holder to the rack. Attach the other holders to the remaining rack, using the same methods **(photo B).**

ATTACH THE RACKS & BASE. Set the base with the attached ends flat on your worksurface. Draw reference lines on the base, 5⅜" in from both short

Waste-basket

A unique decorative accent that won't go to waste.

S ure, you probably don't give wastebaskets a second thought, but they do play an important, if often overlooked, role in every home. When a small trash bin is needed for occasional paper items, you don't want or need a giant, heavy-duty receptacle in the middle of your den. But if you go to the store to buy a wastebasket, often your only options are molded, plastic containers. This project is simple, fun to make and guaranteed to be useful.

The feature that stands out the most on the wastebasket is the use of decorative diagonal kerfs, or slots, cut into the oak plywood sides. It's an easy technique to use, and it gives the wastebasket a customized look. We also planed the legs on the edges to soften the overall appearance and eliminate any sharp edges. A plywood bottom is fit into the project, which is designed to hold a 9"-dia. paint can or a plastic trash bag as a liner.

This is a great little project that adds character to any den or family room setting. Compact, friendly looking and unobtrusive, this wastebasket will keep paper mess in one spot and reduce clutter, while brightening an otherwise forgotten corner of the home.

CONSTRUCTION MATERIALS

Quantity	Lumber
1	¾" × 4 × 4' red oak plywood
1	1½ × 1½" × 6' red oak
1	¾ × ¾" × 3' pine stop molding

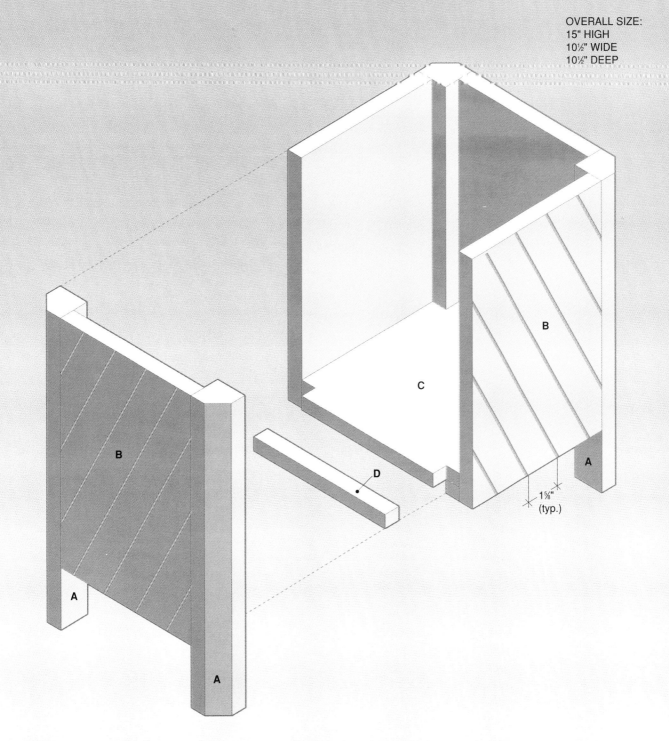

OVERALL SIZE:
15" HIGH
10½" WIDE
10½" DEEP

B

C

D

A

B

A

A

1⅝"
(typ.)

	Cutting List			
Key	**Part**	**Dimension**	**Pcs.**	**Material**
A	Leg	1½ × 1½ × 15"	4	Oak
B	Side panel	¾ × 7½ × 12"	4	Oak plywood

	Cutting List			
Key	**Part**	**Dimension**	**Pcs.**	**Material**
C	Bottom	¾ × 9 × 9"	1	Oak plywood
D	Cleat	¾ × ¾ × 7½"	4	Stop molding

Materials: wood glue, 4d finish nails, ¾" oak edge tape (6'), finishing materials.

Note: Measurements reflect the actual thickness of dimensional lumber.

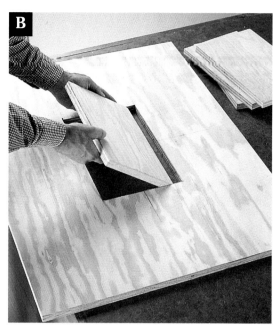

Use a plane to trim away one edge of each leg.

Use a piece of ¾" plywood with an opening the same size as a side panel as a jig for cutting kerfs.

Directions: Wastebasket

MAKE THE LEGS. Each wastebasket leg is trimmed on one edge for a decorative look. Cut the legs (A) to size from red oak 2 × 2, and sand smooth. To angle the trim cuts on the legs, use a combination square to mark lines ¾" down from one corner along two adjacent sides of each leg. Clamp a leg to your worksurface, and then use a sharp plane to remove wood evenly from the edges **(photo A).** Use a belt sander with a medium-grit sanding belt to remove the wood up to the lines and to smooth out the plane marks.

MAKE THE SIDE PANELS. Cut the side panels (B) to size from ¾"-thick oak plywood. Be careful to make sure the panels all are square and uniform in size.

MAKE THE KERF JIG. The decorative kerf cuts on the side panels are made with a circular saw and a simple jig that holds each panel for accurate cutting. The jig is made from a piece of scrap plywood approximately 24 × 32" with a cutout the size of a side panel in the center. To make the jig, center a side panel on the scrap plywood, trace around it and make the cutout with a jig saw **(photo B).**

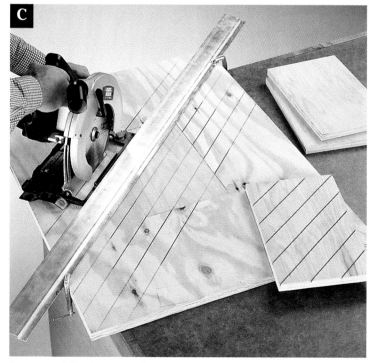

Use a straightedge to guide your circular saw as you make the kerf cuts in the jig and side panels.

LAY OUT THE KERF LINES. Draw cutting lines for the decorative kerfs across both the panel and the jig. To give the side panels a more interesting appearance, we cut two panels with parallel kerfs that run upward from left to right, and two

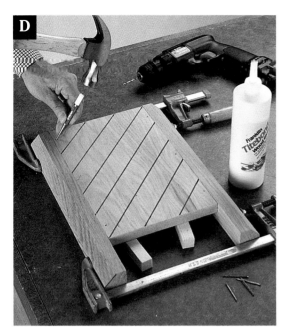

Drill pilot holes, then glue and toenail the side panels to the legs.

As you assemble the wastebasket, check frequently to make sure it's square.

with kerfs that run upward from right to left. This causes the kerfs to form peaks where the adjacent sides meet. To draw the cutting lines, set a side panel into the jig and mark points at 1⅝" intervals along the bottom edge of the panel. Draw cutting lines at a 45° angle to the bottom edge, extending the lines all the way across the panel and the jig (measure at several places to make sure all the lines are parallel). Mark each panel individually, remembering to change the direction of the lines for two of the panels.

CUT THE KERFS. Place a side panel into the jig. Clamp a long straightedge to the jig so the saw blade lines up with one cutting line. Set the blade depth at ¼", then cut along the cutting line, making sure to start and finish the cut well past the edges of the side panel. Moving the straightedge to follow the cutting lines, cut kerfs in all four side panels **(photo C).** After all side panels have been cut, use a household iron

to apply strips of self-adhesive oak veneer edge tape to the top and bottom edges of each side. Trim the edges of the tape with a utility knife when cool. Practice assembling the side panels into a box until you've figured out the pattern of the alternating panels (see *Diagram*, page 89).

ATTACH THE LEGS & SIDES. Cut the cleats (D) to size. Lay one of the side panels on top of two ¾" spacers (the cleats will work), and butt a leg against each edge. Glue and clamp the pieces together. Drill pilot holes, and toenail 4d finish nails through the side and into the legs **(photo D).** Repeat this procedure with the matching side, making sure that the pattern of the kerf cuts runs the same way. Attach the cleats to the side panels, flush with the bottom of each side panel (where the legs overhang), using glue and 4d finish nails.

ASSEMBLE THE WASTEBASKET. Assemble the basket by joining the side panels to the legs and

toenailing all the unfastened joints. Make sure the project is square **(photo E),** and that the faces of the side panels are flush with the outside of the legs. Glue and toenail the joints together with finish nails. Cut the bottom (C) to size, and cut ¾ × ¾" notches into each corner, so it will fit into the opening formed by the sides and legs. Apply glue to the tops of the cleats, and insert the bottom panel.

APPLY FINISHING TOUCHES. Sand any remaining rough edges smooth with fine-grit sandpaper. Be careful not to sand through any veneer on the side edges. Finish as desired. We left the wood unstained and applied two coats of satin-gloss polyurethane.

TIP

When planing wood, you may find that the wood can be worked more easily when planing with the grain. Don't try to remove too much wood at one time; smooth, easy strokes will achieve the best results.

Futon Frame

*A comfortable sofa by day, this futon frame converts easily
into a spare bed frame for overnight guests.*

If you've put off buying a futon because the frames are expensive and complicated to use, wait no more. Designed to hold a full-size futon mattress, our futon frame is built entirely of inexpensive pine. The result is an incredibly sturdy, reliable frame at a fraction of the cost of commercial frames. Instead of the complicated hardware that adds so much to the cost of most futon frames, we developed a trouble-free system of folding frames that attach to one another with heavy-duty hinges. You won't even need to move the futon mattress to turn your sofa into a bed. By day, the futon is a casual sofa for reading or relaxing. When bedtime rolls around, simply slide the seat frame forward to convert your futon sofa into a sturdy, full-size bed your guests will love.

CONSTRUCTION MATERIALS

Quantity	Lumber
12	2 × 4" × 8' pine
7	1 × 6" × 8' pine

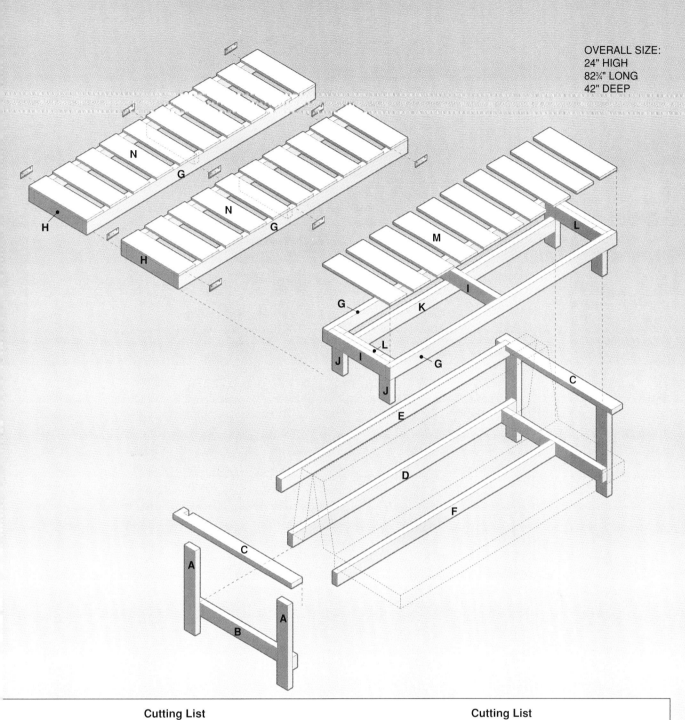

OVERALL SIZE:
24" HIGH
82¾" LONG
42" DEEP

Cutting List

Key	Part	Dimension	Pcs.	Material
A	Post	1½ × 3½ × 23¼"	4	Pine
B	Outer rail	1½ × 3½ × 34"	2	Pine
C	Armrest	1½ × 3½ × 38½"	2	Pine
D	Back rail	1½ × 3½ × 75¾"	1	Pine
E	Backrest	1½ × 3½ × 78¾"	1	Pine
F	Cross rail	1½ × 3½ × 72¾"	1	Pine
G	Frame rail	1½ × 3½ × 75"	6	Pine

Cutting List

Key	Part	Dimension	Pcs.	Material
H	Back stretcher	1½ × 3½ × 16"	6	Pine
I	Seat stretcher	1½ × 3½ × 19"	3	Pine
J	Leg	1½ × 3½ × 11½"	4	Pine
K	Leg stretcher	1½ × 3½ × 69"	2	Pine
L	Leg brace	1½ × 3½ × 12"	2	Pine
M	Seat slat	¾ × 5½ × 22"	10	Pine
N	Back slat	¾ × 5½ × 19"	20	Pine

Materials: Wood screws (#6 × 2", #6 × 2½"), wood glue, 3 x 3" butt hinges (12), nylon furniture glides (8), finishing materials.

Note: Measurements reflect the actual thickness of dimensional lumber.

Use a wood file to make clean, straight edges on the notches in the armrest.

Directions: Futon Frame

MAKE THE ARMRESTS. The futon frame is essentially a combination of four 2 × 4 frames that work together. The outer frame supports all the other frames. This frame stays in place while the futon is folded or unfolded. The armrests are notched at the back end to hold the backrest. All the rest of the parts are simply cut to length, drilled and sanded. Counterbore all the visible screw holes for ⅜"-diameter plugs. Cut the armrests (C). The armrests attach to the tops of the posts with glue and screws. They are notched to hold the backrest. To mark the notches, lay the armrests together edge to edge. Draw a 1½" square along the inside edge of each armrest, starting 1½" in from one end. Cut the notches with a jig saw. To get a tight-fitting notch, cut just inside the cutting lines, then use a wood file to remove the last fraction of wood and clean up the cuts **(photo A).**

ASSEMBLE THE ARMREST FRAMES. Cut the posts (A) and outer rails (B) to length. Use a pad sander with medium-grit paper to remove splinters, smooth out rough spots, and sand away any grading stamps. The outer rails fit across the inside faces of the posts to support the back frames when the futon frame is unfolded. To mark reference lines for the outer rails on the posts, lay the posts side by side in pairs with the ends flush. Draw lines across the pairs of posts, 8" from the bottom ends. Position the outer rails against the posts so the top edges of the rails are on the lines and the ends of the rails are flush with the sides of the posts. Apply glue to the joints and secure them with 2½" screws. If glue oozes from the joints, let it dry and scrape it away later with a chisel. While the glue is drying on the rails and posts, prepare the armrests. Attach an armrest atop each pair of posts so the inside edges are flush. The back edge of the rear post should be flush with the front of the notch and the front post should be 1½" from the front of the armrest. Use glue and 2½" screws to secure the armrests to the posts **(photo B).**

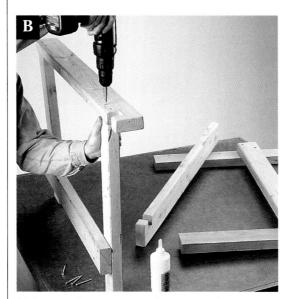

Make sure the armrest notches are on the same side of the posts as the outer rails.

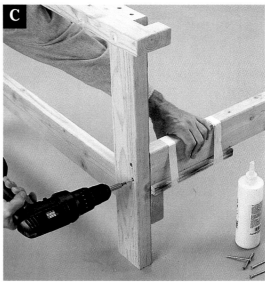

Tape a ¾"-thick spacer to the bottom edge of the back rail to create a gap between the back rail and the outer rail.

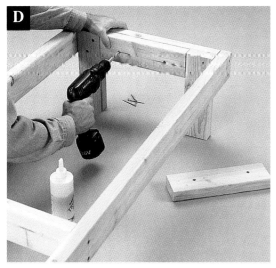

The leg braces hold the the legs firmly against the frame rails to prevent wobble.

Space the slats in the seat frame so the gaps align with the back frame.

COMPLETE THE OUTER FRAME. Cut the back rail (D), backrest (E) and cross rail (F) to length. Tape a ¾"-thick piece of scrap to the bottom edge at each end of the back rail. The scraps are spacers that will hold the back rail at the correct height as it's fastened between the rear posts. Drill counterbored pilot holes for #6 screws centered along the back edge of the rear post, 9¾" and 11¼" from the bottom. Apply glue to an end of the back rail and rest the spacer on the outer rail. Support the back rail level and flush with the back edge of the post, then drive 2½" screws through the post to secure the back rail **(photo C),** and remove the spacers. Fasten the other end of the rail. Next, fasten the backrest in place. Drill a pilot hole near each end of the backrest ¾" from the end and ¾" up from the bottom edge. Brush glue sparingly inside the notches, then slide the backrest along the post and up into the notches until the top edges are flush. Drive screws through the pilot holes in the

backrest, then add deeply counterbored screws driven through the sides of the armrests into each end of the backrest. Finally, fasten the cross rail between the outer rails, 17" from the rear posts, using glue and counterbored screws. Glue wood plugs into all the visible counterbore holes and sand the outer frame to round the corners and edges.

MAKE THE SEAT FRAME. The seat frame carries most of the weight, so it's heavier and has legs. To make the seat frame, cut two frame rails (G), and the seat stretchers (I). Mark the centers of the frame rails. Stand the seat rails on edge, then fasten the seat stretchers between the rails with glue and screws. Fasten a stretcher at each end of the rails, and one in the middle. Cut the legs (J), leg stretchers (K) and leg braces (L). Lightly round the bottoms of the legs. Rounding the bottom edges helps keep the legs from splintering as the futon frame is pushed and pulled to convert it from bed to sofa. When attaching the legs and leg braces, simply countersink

the pilot holes because the screw heads will not be visible. Fasten a leg to each inside corner of the seat frame, using glue and screws. Butt the legs tightly against the corners with the narrow edge of each leg against the seat rail. Keep the tops of the legs flush with the rails. Drive screws through the legs and into the rails to secure them. The leg braces fit tightly between the legs and against the outer seat stretchers to lock the legs into their upright position. Apply glue to the faces of the braces before fastening them between the legs, flush with the tops of the seat stretchers **(photo D).** To further support the legs, drill counterbored pilot holes along the outside edges of each leg, 1" and 2½" from the bottom edges of the seat stretchers. Glue, then fasten, one leg stretcher between the outside edges of the front legs, and another between the back legs just below the seat stretchers to complete the framework for the seat.

MAKE THE BACK FRAMES. The back frames are smaller and lighter than the seat frame. These twin frames will be hinged to the seat frame and rest on the outer rails when the futon is extended for sleeping. Make the back frames in the same manner as the seat frame. For each back frame, cut two frame rails (G) and three back stretchers (H). Fasten the back stretchers between pairs of frame rails, as you did the seat stretchers, to complete the framework for our futon frame.

INSTALL THE SLATS & HINGES. Slats and hinges are all that remain to be attached to the frames. Cut the seat slats (M) and back slats (N). Starting with the back frames, fasten a slat across each end of the frame with glue and 2" screws. Space the remaining slats evenly, about 2¼" apart, then fasten them in place with counterbored screws and glue. Attach the seat slats **(photo E).** The futon frame should be completely assembled before the finish is applied to make sure the frames work together properly. Any adjustments that might be needed at this point will not

require refinishing. To test-assemble the futon frame, turn one back frame facedown, slat to slat, over the seat frame so the back edges are flush. Attach heavy-duty 3 × 3" hinges across the frames so the barrels are centered on the joint between the back slats and seat slats. Mount hinges 2" from each end, with two more spaced evenly between them. Mount four more hinges to one side of the remaining back frame so the barrels are flush with the top of the slats. Lay the outer frame on its back, then attach the back frame to the inside edge of the back rail using the hinges. Stand the frame up and slide the seat into place. Tip the two back frames together to install the remaining hinges **(photo F).** Test the operation of the hinges, adjust or realign them, if needed, then remove all the hinges until the finish has been applied.

APPLY FINISHING TOUCHES. Apply your finish of choice before you fasten the frames together permanently. Glue and plug all the counterbored holes in the frames and slats. When the glue is dry, sand the slats and frames to produce smooth surfaces for your finish. Start with medium-grit paper and a belt sander to quickly level the plugs. Finish-sand with fine or extra-fine paper. Wipe clean, then apply your finish. We used tung oil because it creates a durable finish that penetrates the wood and is easy to renew when repairing scratches. Apply the finish and allow plenty of drying time. Reinstall the hinges, and add nylon furniture glides to the bottoms of the legs and posts. To open the futon frame, simply pull the seat forward. Pull up on the joint between the two back frames to turn the bed back into a sofa.

Install hinges between the back frames with the futon frame in the closed (sofa) position.